OUT
SOURCING

OUT
SOURCING

THE DEFINITIVE VIEW, APPLICATIONS, AND IMPLICATIONS

NICHOLAS C. BURKHOLDER

John Wiley & Sons, Inc.

Published by John Wiley & Sons, Inc., Hoboken, New Jersey.
Published simultaneously in Canada.

For general information on our other products and services or for technical
support, please contact our Customer Care Department within the United States
at (800) 762-2974, outside the United States at (317) 572-3993 or fax (317) 572-4002.

Wiley also publishes its books in a variety of electronic formats. Some content that
appears in print may not be available in electronic books. For more information about
Wiley products, visit our web site at www.wiley.com.

Library of Congress Cataloging-in-Publication Data:

Burkholder, Nicholas C.
    Outsourcing : the definitive view, applications, and implications / Nicholas C.
Burkholder.
        p. cm.
    Includes index.
    ISBN-13: 978-0-471-69481-6 (cloth)
    ISBN-10: 0-471-69481-9 (cloth)
    1. Contracting out. I. Title.   MAR '07
HD2365.B87 2005
658.4'058—dc22   2005048986

Printed in the United States of America.

10 9 8 7 6 5 4 3 2 1

To the individual worker, the ultimate resource

And

O. Craig Burkholder, John F. Burkholder, and Paul J. Burkholder,

*three exceptional workers whom I admire greatly
and from whom I have learned much*

Contents

CONTENTS

Introduction

Outsourcing is one of the oldest hot business ideas. It was used the first time a carpenter paid someone else to cut down a tree for wood. The first significant organizational outsourcing was for the most brutal of work: waging war. Carl von Clausewitz, the early-nineteenth-century military strategist, noted in *On War* that as gold replaced strategic obligations "armies were turned into mercenaries." Outsourcing, whether in the form of call centers or soldiers of fortune, is simply a classic economic principle—division of labor—taken to its logical conclusion: a virtual assembly line in a global factory. The benefits, then, are obvious; a business that reduces operating costs and increases efficiency can lower prices for its consumers and increase investment, which, in turn, creates new, often higher-paying jobs.

There is nothing novel about outsourcing. Indeed, management experts have been proclaiming the benefits of outsourcing for decades. In 1990, organization expert Charles Handy introduced his idea of a trifoliate "Shamrock Organization": (1) a small permanent core of management and technical employees, (2) a flexible labor force of part-time and temporary workers, and (3) independent contractors and outside suppliers who are brought in as needed for special and reoccurring projects. Handy recommended that all nonessential work should be contracted out—or outsourced—to workers who specialize in that particular task.

INTRODUCTION

The same year, management guru Tom Peters predicted that we would all become companies of one with cell phones and fax machines in our cars outsourcing work to each other. The Internet has accelerated and expanded the workplace that Handy and Peters spoke of. It has also fundamentally changed the ways in which we can work.

In today's globalized economy, it is impossible not to outsource. As Tom Friedman says, the world is flat and we are all working in the same factory. Every organization outsources; the only question is how effectively. The venerable publisher of this book outsourced the typesetting and printing of this book (in order, we hope, to sell the book at a price low enough to entice potential buyers). Thousands of contractors are available to provide services for virtually every function. Even unions participate. Utilities and other organizations outsource most electrical power work to contractors who in turn outsource to the International Brotherhood of Electrical Workers (IBEW). The IBEW selects, constantly trains, and manages a workforce of highly skilled linemen for this very technical and dangerous work.

And yet, to say that outsourcing is ubiquitous and inevitable is not the same as saying it is desirable or virtuous. CEOs are concerned about public perception of any outsourcing decision, particularly offshoring. CFOs are concerned about costs and risk management. And just about everyone else is concerned about their jobs. Like reengineering, outsourcing can devastate the lives of thousands of workers. There are also implications for the people and communities to which work is outsourced. All of these considerations are part of the complete outsourcing equation.

Organizations outsource for a myriad of reasons. Some say they outsource to other countries because the United States' litigious culture creates unbearable compliance costs. For example,

Introduction

The Wall Street Journal recently reported that some Indian outsourcing companies are seeing business rise more than 50 percent per year because of costs related to Sarbanes-Oxley.[1] Also, some businesses seek to reduce other high employment costs, such as wages, benefits, and unemployment insurance. General Motors says that outsourcing can help it control health-care costs, the top priority of its chairman. Other CFOs have told us that they will look to offshore higher-paying positions if the compensation ceiling for Social Security contributions is raised.

Although many businesses seek lower costs, some also seek better workers. It is no secret that American students lag behind their Asian peers in math and science. Many businesses outsource simply because the work force in India or China may be better educated, more motivated, and cheaper to boot. For a business manager, this seems an easy decision.

The financial markets also exert a very powerful influence. Staffing.org contacted more than 100 organizations that announced layoffs after the dot-com bubble burst. The use of contractors and contingent workers actually increased in most of these organizations, yet Wall Street invariably considered the layoffs a positive indicator. It is also clear that the analysts favor organizations that outsource.

Organizations also outsource out of fear of falling behind. In *The Witch Doctors* (Three Rivers Press, 1998) John Micklethwait and Adrian Wooldridge write of executives who flock to one management theory after another in an eternal quest for the latest and best practice. Buzzwords echo in boardrooms around the globe without any consideration of validity. As Daniel

---

[1]Eric Bellman, "Tracking the Numbers/Outside Audit: One More Cost of Sarbanes-Oxley; Outsourcing to India," *Wall Street Journal*, July 14, 2005, C1.

INTRODUCTION

Drezner explains in "Outsourcing the Boogeyman" (foreign affairs.org, May/June 2004), "Much of the perceived boom in outsourcing stems from companies' eagerness to latch onto the latest management trends. . . . Many will partially reverse course once the hidden costs of offshore outsourcing become apparent." Not surprisingly, some theories actually prove to be deleterious to organization performance. For example, the reengineering craze actually wreaked havoc on organizations and individuals. Outsourcing, then, must be judged on its own merits rather than being viewed as a miracle cure for a company's ills.

One of the best-selling books on outsourcing is Peter Bendor-Samuel's *Turning Lead into Gold* (Executive Excellence Publishing, 2000). The title comes from the ultimate goal of alchemy, the medieval pseudoscientific forerunner of chemistry. But just as nothing turns lead into gold, outsourcing is not a magic shortcut to unlimited profits. The decision to outsource, like any business decision, must be rational and calculated, based on empirical evidence and not just the latest fad.

Staffing.org, a nonprofit that fosters the use of measurement to make the best decisions about people and work, has been collecting recruiting performance data since 1999. Its analysis of almost 3,000 U.S.-based organizations clearly indicates that there is no correlation between performance and whether the recruiting function is internal or outsourced.

When we originally conceived this book, our intention was to provide a definitive study of outsourcing. That role now seems academic. Instead we're offering practical perspectives and solutions for a very changed world; a world in which work can be instantly and seamlessly moved around the globe, a world in which past Employment Management Association president and Monsanto vice president John Kitson says the very nature of work has changed: "It's not about loyalty, relationships, or even a commitment toward common goals. It's about getting the job done."

We're also committed to taking Albert Einstein's advice that "Everything should be made as simple as possible, but not simpler." To that end we have shared the best information on outsourcing and summarized our most important findings in the case studies of Chapter 3, Imperatives. These case studies on subjects as varied as today's small business and the health care industry follow to illustrate the points found in Chapter 3. This will give a broader perspective on just how involved outsourcing is in our everyday lives.

What Is Outsourcing?

The debate about outsourcing is hampered by the fact that people are often unclear about the subject. What exactly is outsourcing? According to Wikipedia, outsourcing is "the delegation of non-core operations or jobs from internal production to an external entity (such as a subcontractor) that specializes in that operation." Outsourcing, then, is hardly a new or radical business practice. Offshoring, a specific subset of outsourcing, involves the practice of moving noncore operations overseas, either by transferring jobs to a foreign subcontractor or building a facility where labor is cheap. When politicians raise the specter of a "race to the bottom," they are referring to offshoring. Although there are plenty of myths surrounding the practice of outsourcing, the facts are readily available, and they argue overwhelmingly in favor of it.

THE MYTHS AND FACTS OF OUTSOURCING

Patricia J. Moser
Vice President and Chief Procurement Officer
Rogers Communications Inc.

As consumers we are continuously engaged in outsourcing. We hire painters, plumbers, gardeners, and mechanics. Some may retort by stating that they, in fact, perform many of these activities themselves, but they are in the minority. Anyone who has ever looked at a professionally painted home or landscaped lawn and compared it to the do-it-yourself variety would likely agree that the quality and timeliness associated with the professionally performed work far exceeds that of do-it-yourselfer.

They said, why is it that, when it comes to reviewing our business processes, organizations often balk at the thought of outsourcing? Fear mostly. The thought of losing control and the belief that many of the myths surrounding outsourcing are fact have kept many from even considering outsourcing.

The reality is that organizations that embrace outsourcing and leverage their resources to focus on their core business will continue to be the market leaders of tomorrow. So before you consider running for the hills at the mention of outsourcing, let's separate the myths from the facts.

Myth: Outsourcing a function means that the company does not consider it critical to its success.

Fact: Businesses often outsource functions that they define as critical to their success.

According to the Outsourcing Institute, more than 30 percent of companies today are engaged in some form of outsourcing. Consider how many firms have outsourced information technology, or the major automobile firms that outsource much of their manufacturing. Aren't car-engine components critical to an automobile company's product performance and, thus, its reputation? Isn't data and information flow critical to the success of all corporations? Critical and core functions are not mutually inclusive. In fact, it is the visionary corporation that understands that it may not have the expertise, resources, or strategic focus on a critical function and that having the services provided by a world-class outsourcer can significantly enhance them.

Myth: Outsourcing can cost more when considering factors beyond head-count reduction.

Fact: If head-count reduction is the only focus of an outsourcing activity, then it is doomed to failure.

When determining the relevancy of proceeding with outsourcing a function, a total cost evaluation must be considered. When outsourcing a function, significant opportunities for cost savings exist. For example, with experience and knowledge of best practices, the outsourcer can review the complete business cycle and deliver ongoing, best-in-class value; the outsourcer can benefit from leveraged knowledge gleaned through other engagements by the outsourcer, enhance control over internal maverick activities, and avoid the need for capital investments for new technology and the like while having access to the latest tools.

Obviously some aspect of this would be in the pricing of

the outsourced contract. However, as such, it is, in most cases, an operating expense and, therefore, the cost is less as a result of the outsourcer leveraging this technology over several enterprises.

Outsourcing can result in a company quickly reaping benefits through expertise, enhanced control, and leverage with limited capital investment and with reduced operational expenses.

Myth: An outsourcer will not be motivated by the same business drivers as an internal group to ensure customer focus and maintain flexibility in a changing market.

Fact: Whether you purchase a product, a service, or outsourcing, it is crucial that you as the customer set the ground rules and negotiate service-level agreements in which expectations and targets are stated and regular business review meetings are conducted to ensure that the supplier is measuring up.

Internal politics or other bureaucratic issues that an internal group is often faced with, or the potential budgetary constraints that often hamper progress or restrain flexibility, do not restrict the outsourcer. The supplier of outsourced services is there to support the client and to assist the client in meeting its goals and objectives. There is usually much greater conflict between internal resources than there is between a client and a supplier whose long-term relationship and payment depends on the customer's satisfaction.

Myth: Career growth and opportunities are limited or nonexistent for outsourced staff.

Fact: Career growth and opportunities abound when an individual joins an outsourcer.

For the outsourcer, the outsourced function is its core business, not just a critical element to success. When staff is migrated to an outsourcer, these employees have now joined a firm that specializes in the activity that they had been performing internally. In their own organizations, they may have encountered internal career paralysis because of limited options for growth available in their chosen field. When joining an outsourcer, there are constantly new clients, new engagements, and new opportunities for growth. The employee of an outsourcer becomes a sales professional and consultant responsible for client delivery, as well as client satisfaction.

It is critical that the outsourcer is leading-edge, whether in technology or in business processes, because this is part of the value proposition provided to potential clients. Areas such as training become a core element in employee development and a key criterion in ongoing success of the business.

Myths are created as a result of fear and of trying to develop one's own interpretation of the situation given that fear, so stop corporately milking the cow and growing the wheat. Isn't it easier just to go to the grocery store?

Case Study: The Federal Government— An Outsourcing Organization

The federal government has practiced outsourcing in one form or another for many years. Although not traditionally referring to the practice as outsourcing, government agencies and commercial organizations have long contracted out blue collar administrative- and maintenance-type functions, such as equipment and grounds maintenance and custodial, laundry, and food services. These were functions that the outsourcing organization had neither the skill sets nor the internal resources to perform.

In the private sector, the move to make America more competitive in the global markets forced corporations to focus on their own core competencies. This focus led to the outsourcing of functions that did not directly add value to their competitive-edge areas. Functions that were outsourced evolved to include a number of white-collar type functions, such as:

- Business services (including business support services, electronic imaging, and records management).
- Logistics (including import/export services, freight brokers, freight audit services, and warehousing).
- Human resources (including payroll management, tax administration, benefits management, workers' compensation, and staffing support).
- Health care (including specialized medical departments in hospitals, support services for hospitals, clinical services, and business services).

The commercial information technology (IT) world has followed much the same path. Initially, most outsourcing of IT included functions that could be narrowly and easily defined. In the 1970s and most of the 1980s, the majority of outsourced IT work was for low-end services, such as tape cleaning and keypunching. More complex tasks were handled by in-house IT shops.

However, outsourcing significantly impacted the IT world in a major way in the late 1980s. At that time, Kodak selected three companies to perform a significant part of its internal information systems activities. As a result, IT organizations across the country considered outsourcing functions such as facility management and payroll processing.

OUTSOURCING

As with other organizational functions, IT organizations began scrutinizing their competitiveness, including focusing on their own core competencies. Organizational leaders even began to challenge the assumption that IT itself is a legitimate core organizational competency. As a result, outsourcing of government IT functions now includes work that only a few years ago was considered so critically related to the agency mission that it mandated performance by government employees.

This dramatic increase in outsourcing of IT functions has become big business in both private and government sectors. IT outsourcing is now being employed by every sector of business and government worldwide. IT functions are being outsourced by American cities, states, and federal agencies, as well as international agencies, governments, and the private sector. Internationally, Canada, Australia, and Great Britain have all outsourced significant IT functions.

Since the mid-1950s, the United States' official policy has been to acquire needed goods and services from commercial sources. In 1955, President Dwight D. Eisenhower stated, "The federal government will not start or carry out any commercial activity to provide a service or product for its own use if such product or service can be procured from private enterprise through ordinary business channels."

THE FEDERAL GOVERNMENT'S ADVICE: WHEN TO OUTSOURCE (OR, HOW DID IT WORK FOR THEM?)

Successful outsourcing enables organizations to focus on what they do best—accomplish their mission. For the federal government, it is the core business of governing and government. Information technology is, in many cases, an important part of an agency's operation, but it is seldom its core expertise, that is, it is not what the agency is in business to do. To redirect this focus, federal agencies are analyzing the extent to which IT represents a strategic aspect of their operation, and if their internal capability is likely to provide the high-quality results necessary for success.

Outsourcing is not an end in itself. It is a management tool and should be approached in that manner. In determining whether to outsource, management will make numerous decisions that have significant consequences. In the course of the outsourcing process, management must address several critical issues in order to achieve success. These issues include identifying potential organizational problems, factoring in human resources and behavior, considering asset transfers and authorities, establishing and negotiating contracts, and overcoming political obstacles. These issues are key reasons that mandate top management's involvement throughout the entire process.

REASONS WHY A FEDERAL AGENCY MIGHT USE OUTSOURCING

Private industry and the federal government have numerous reasons for outsourcing. Based on a survey by the General Services Administration in February 1998, "Outsourcing Information Technology," here are the reasons, in descending order of importance, for outsourcing information systems:

- Focus in-house resources on core functions.
- Allow personnel cost savings.
- Improve quality of information systems services.
- Increase flexibility.

- Increase access to new technology.
- Provide alternatives to in-house costs.
- Stabilize information-systems costs.
- Achieve technology cost savings.
- Reengineer processes.
- Reduce technological obsolescence risk.

Federal managers have similar reasons for outsourcing. These reasons can be combined and categorized as follows:

- Budget realities.
- Cost reduction.
- Access to skilled personnel.
- Improved IT responsiveness.
- Help with legacy systems.
- Improved business and customer service.
- Implementation of new architecture.

CHALLENGES FACED BY SOME FEDERAL AGENCIES WHEN THEY BEGAN OUTSOURCING

Once the decision to pursue outsourcing has been made, management and the outsourcing study team will be faced with numerous challenges. Political opposition to the potential outsourcing may come from internal sources, unions, community leaders, and possibly other contractors, who may be affected by the outsourcing decision. Senior management should communicate with internal or external groups. This communication should begin as early in the process as possible and continue periodically.

Developing the government's cost proposal can be a challenge. The outsourcing team will need detailed costs that normally are not readily available, such as personnel costs that are adjusted for items such as fringe benefits (workers' compensation, bonuses, awards, and vacation pay); retirement (which may vary by occupation); employee insurance; and Medicare contributions. In addition to personnel costs, all expenses for materials and supplies must be accounted for. Further adjustments must be made for overhead (other than fringe benefits) and general and administrative costs. Finally, inflation adjustments must also be made.

ACHIEVING SUCCESS— HOW FEDERAL AGENCIES WIN

Once the decision to pursue an outsourcing project has been made, the acquisition strategy becomes key. Success in outsourcing is dependent on creating a win-win situation that requires clearly defined expectations and flexibility on the part of both parties. In addition, it requires use of an appropriate contract type that provides an incentive to the vendor to continually improve service and to work with the outsourcing organization as a team.

Many agencies are quietly outsourcing services. As budgets continue to shrink, agencies are searching for ways to continue to provide quality service to their customers. One way to do this has been to write labor hour/time and material contracts, purchase orders, or delivery orders for a small number of positions. By contracting for small, additional amounts of work each time, agencies can meet their needs without formal or complex outsourcing studies. The rapid expansion and increased availability of government-wide acquisition contracts (GWACs) has accelerated this trend.

Creation of a win-win scenario between the government and the contractor is perhaps the most significant factor leading to the successful implementation of an outsourcing strategy. Flexibility is the key to creating the win-win scenario, and the key to flexibility is communication.

Agencies and contractors must enter into an arrangement in which constant dialogue is the norm. Agencies that look upon a contract as an inflexible and unchangeable document do themselves as well as the contractor a disservice. Good communication between the parties to the contract (these include the end user, the program management staff if different than the end user, the contracting staff, and the contractor) can be facilitated by the use of an integrated-process team (IPT) or a customer process-improvement working group (CPIWG). These groups would meet regularly to identify and solve problems, propose innovative management and technical approaches, improve processes, and implement commercial practices.

Another way to implement a win-win situation is to find methods of compensating contractors that produce big savings to the agency. These savings can be achieved through various means such as the introduction of new technology, the reengineering of certain time-consuming but key processes, the introduction of program and risk management methodologies, and so forth. Agencies can provide incentives to contractors through incentive or award fee contracts. Under such arrangements, agencies should set the additional fees to be gained by the contractors at a level that truly will incentivize the contractors to risk their own funds to achieve a high quality of service. In addition, the agency will want to make sure that contractor management is aware of the incentive or award fees and the importance the government places on the service received.

Even the Government Makes Mistakes: What Happens When Outsourcing Is Not the Answer?

There will always be some situations that do not lead to satisfactory results. Even successful contracts will have to be put out to bid periodically, usually as the result of an expiring contract term. The agency may have developed better information, metrics, and the like, with which it can enhance the new solicitation.

Outsourcing will grow to be an accepted way of doing business as both the private sector and government agencies focus more directly on customer service and cost/budget reductions. As the concept becomes more accepted and outsourcing opportunities expand, the process will be more clearly outlined. Federal agencies will accept outsourcing as another tool to improve services and reduce costs.

CHAPTER 2

Who Is Outsourcing?

Everyone Is Doing It: An Overview of the Companies That Outsource

If you were to give a pop quiz and ask most Americans just how extensively outsourcing is used today, most of those people would fail. Although outsourcing makes the headlines in the daily newspaper and the lead story on the local news, it is a confusing issue at best. Perhaps that is because companies are sending mixed signals about outsourcing. A recent *Wall Street Journal* headline (June 16, 2005) reported "Firms Expect to Increase IT Outsourcing," but this was followed by a seemingly contradictory subheading: "Executives Report Dissatisfaction, Especially With Offshore Providers." According to the article, while 74 percent of executives expect to increase the use of outsourcing services, a full 51 percent of executives ended an outsourcing relationship early in the preceding year. It seems that businesses are still learning the ropes when it comes to outsourcing. Although this is cause for caution, it should not deter companies from making the right decisions for themselves. There is a certain optimism inherent in these statistics, because even many of the executives who have had poor outsourcing relationships expect to increase their outsourcing-related activities. Outsourcing is here to stay.

POLL OF GLOBAL EXECUTIVES ON OUTSOURCING

A survey of 7,300 senior executives around the world by consultant McKinsey & Company found that four out of five executives think outsourcing is good for the global economy (*McKinsey Quarterly*, January 2004; www.mckinsey.com/mgi/ie/offshoring). Split by continent, the ratio was the same for executives in Europe, Asia, and the United States, the survey said.

When queried on the implications of outsourcing on their own businesses, though 70 percent of the Europeans approved, 97 percent of Indians also approved, as did 86 percent of Chinese. However, the figure fell in the United States, home to the world's most globalized companies. Only 58 percent of the U.S. executives were positive on the development.

On the global economy, the executives were cautiously optimistic, and most of them thought it was healthier than it was six months earlier, but they saw the improvement leveling off by mid-2005. They viewed Asia as the region with the most promising growth prospects for 2005.

Executives of smaller companies said hunting for talent and capital were their main worries, whereas executives of larger ones were concerned that consumers would rein in spending. They also felt policies on foreign direct investment were critical, especially to executives in developing economies.

The survey, conducted in January 2004 polled leaders from a wide range of industries and regions to develop a worldwide barometer of executive sentiment on economic and business trends. About 12 percent of those surveyed were chief executives from 115 countries.

A confidence index derived from the survey registered a level of 67 on a scale of 100, where 50 or more indicated optimism. Executives in developing markets had a confidence index of 71, indicating they were more bullish than the overall survey average.

Executives in China and India were more optimistic than their peers in the rest of the world, with 87 percent and 80 percent, respectively, predicting the economic climate would get even better by July. Of the other executives surveyed, 73 percent shared that sentiment.

Although executives were optimistic, they didn't see an easy road ahead. In most regions, the economy was the top concern for the executives.

The exception was the emerging markets regions, where executives were focused on the search for talent.

Beyond the economy, executives of larger companies worried about the sustainability of consumer spending—considered the lifeline that kept the recent U.S. economic downturn from becoming still worse—followed by the competition for talent. Many also listed currency fluctuations, pricing, and global competition as key concerns. Executives from smaller companies, however, believed that hiring and retaining talent was the second most important concern after the economy. Access to capital, which executives at larger companies hardly noticed, came in third.

Perhaps not surprisingly, executives in developing markets

were more bullish than were their counterparts in developed markets about the benefits, for companies and the world economy, of outsourcing manufacturing and business processes to low-wage countries.

In order to stay competitive in today's global marketplace, companies of all sizes are realizing that outsourcing must be an option for them. They recognize the potential benefits of turning certain operations over to outside parties, whether the work ends up being done down the hall, up the street, or across the ocean. Business leaders and owners are usually the first to understand the basic reason for outsourcing: *It reduces costs*.

And what happens when a business can reduce costs? It becomes more efficient; it has more capital to invest (which ultimately will create more jobs in the near future); and it becomes more competitive. In the same McKinsey survey, over 50 percent of executives reported that reducing costs was their number one reason for beginning an outsourcing program at their company.

SHORT ON PRIESTS, U.S. CATHOLICS OUTSOURCE PRAYERS TO INDIAN CLERGY (FROM WIRE SERVICE REPORTS)

With Roman Catholic clergy in short supply in the United States, Indian priests are picking up some of their work, saying Mass for special intentions, in a sacred, if unusual, version of outsourcing. American, as well as Canadian and European churches, are sending Mass intentions, or requests for services like these, to remember deceased relatives and thanksgiving prayers, to clergy in

India. About 2 percent of India's more than one billion people are Christians, most of them Catholics. Although most requests are made via mail or personally through traveling clergy, a significant number arrive via e-mail, a sign that technology is expediting this practice.

HUMAN RESOURCES OUTSOURCING CONTINUES TO GROW AMONG COMPANIES SEEKING TO REDUCE COSTS AND IMPROVE SERVICE LEVELS

Human resources outsourcing increases throughout 2005. Global competition, pricing, and improved service levels are driving factors motivating companies to outsource noncore functions such as HR.

Dallas, TX (PRWeb) March 22, 2005—HR outsourcing is becoming the most outsourced business process according to recent data provided by Gartner. Projected forecasts show that HR outsourcing is growing at an annual rate of 8.6 percent a year and will grow to almost $40 billion by 2007. Additionally, Gartner estimates that 85 percent of U.S. enterprises will outsource at least one component of their HR functions by the end of 2005.

"We are seeing a lot of activity in the telecommunications, retail, and government sectors," says Ed Rankin, HR business process outsourcing (BPO) practice leader for the outsourcing consulting firm, the Trowbridge Group. "Reducing cost and improving service levels are key motivators for companies to outsource."

According to Rankin, organizations with 10,000+ employees may save as much as 20 percent or more through HR outsourcing.

Organizations that outsource noncore functions such as HR can spend more time on strategic initiatives focused on revenue generation and profitability.

How Outsourcing Increases Profit

Outsourcing is the process in which one business provides specific services and results for another business instead of performing the same services and results themselves. Instead of packaging, handling, and shipping products, a business can outsource this process to a packaging and shipping service.

Opportunities abound in every business to outsource functions such as physically delivering products to customers, handling all of the billing and customer service, preparing governmental reports, handling tax issues and insurance, and all human resources functions. Companies such as NetLedger offer online accounting and general services that eliminate all such in-house functions for a small business.

In essence, you get to use the technologies and expertise of others, thus eliminating your own capital investment and staffing requirements. Many times you can have customized versions of their technologies meet your very specific needs.

If you're a start-up business, this is a great way to reduce your costs. Additional benefits of outsourcing relationships are paying only for the results, components, or products received, the hours worked, the products sold, and so on. Outsourcing allows you to know exactly what each product or result will cost before you decide to obtain it. Using outsourcing allows you to establish a more accurate price for the product or service you deliver because the costs are set in advance and stay that way. You will enjoy prices that will frequently be less than what it would cost to produce the same products, results, and/or services yourself. The good news is that the Internet is making it much easier to find outsourcing partners.

Combining Existing Technologies and Outsourcing to Produce New Products

Cliff Tyner and Larry Nickolson are the owners and entire staff of Applied Science, Inc. (www.applied-science.com), in Grass Valley, California. They design products for other companies. In fact, they created their own very successful new product in their spare time by combining off-the-shelf existing technologies.

According to Cliff, "We produced an accurate, portable, easier to use, yet very safe, monitor for blood donations at half the price. It took us less than six months, versus the normal two-to-three-year period."

As Cliff further explains, "We used many off-the-shelf components, such as a plastic enclosure designed for use as an electronics housing for various meters, a low-cost weight-monitoring device designed for use in electronic postage scales, and a unique power-efficient motor commonly used for battery-powered store displays. A customized PC board and software to control all of the unit's functions (using current technology components) was used to create a cost-effective design and a very marketable blood donor marketing machine."

The unit gives the technicians more freedom and flexibility by monitoring many of the steps required by the Food and Drug Administration (FDA) in the donation process. This was not as easy as it sounds because the machine had to be approved by the FDA, which meant passing the FDA's very stringent specifications.

Cliff and Larry had the subassembly process outsourced, but chose to do the final assembly and testing in house. This allowed them to "personally verify the manufacturability and reliability, by solving or improving the design and manufacturing steps." They closely studied their bigger, more powerful competitors and "learned from them how not to complicate things." Remember, they produced their much better, less-expensive solution by simply using readily available, existing components.

SMART TECHNOLOGY CHOICES CAN GENERATE MORE PROFITS

Identify your needs and find cost-effective technological solutions

Today's technology can add to your profits, as long as you're careful about what you buy and how you adapt it to your business. The fastest and easiest ways to increase your profits are to reduce your costs and/or increase your sales volume.

As a small business owner, you have so many choices and options when it comes to technology. The biggest challenge is choosing and locating the right technology or application for your business. Technology generally helps companies be more efficient. Specifically, it streamlines the sales process; increases efficiencies in the manufacturing or delivering of products and services;

speeds up billing, collection, and customer services functions; and generally provides information on a more timely basis.

It doesn't matter whether you're in the start-up or expansion mode; first you must evaluate the true needs or opportunities that exist in your business. During this phase, check to see what changes are taking place in your industry. Talk to your customers to learn what they might need or want that you're currently not providing. Seek input from employees about ways to improve the process and reduce costs.

Once you know and understand what changes you need to make or results you want to accomplish, then begin searching for the right technologies to accomplish those goals. You will be surprised at the quantity and quality of options available to assist you in reducing your costs and increasing your sales volume. It's amazing how many technologies can be used by one business to perform a function and yet the same technology can be applied to accomplish a different activity in another business.

Be sure to develop a technology strategy that meshes with your overall business goals. If you want to sell on the World Wide Web, then build the infrastructure that allows you to do so. If you're changing a major function such as your billing system, then be sure to test it prior to final conversion. You might find maintaining the same records on two systems during this phase will allow for a smooth transition and avoid potential disasters.

Always build contingency funds into your budget for unanticipated costs or problems. If a project runs short on money or puts too much stress on just a few people, it could fail. Don't forget to budget for the in-house training needs, technical maintenance, user support, prelaunch testing, and any collateral required.

FOUR WAYS OF OBTAINING TECHNOLOGY

Once you have decided what you need, you then have to decide whether and when to purchase, lease, or rent and how to extract the greatest profits possible. To find the right answers to these questions, business owners can consider the following four options:

1. Buy the latest technology and use it to increase profits until the technology no longer produces the desired profits.
2. Buy existing technologies that have been used and tested for years (normally at lesser costs) and organize them in a new way to increase profits.
3. Rent technologies only as needed.
4. Use the technologies owned and operated by others by acquiring the products or services needed from other businesses (called outsourcing).

Small businesses are normally nimble enough to use any of these methods to great advantage.

Buying the latest technologies can be a costly and tricky process because of high costs and the fact that such technologies are frequently not fully tested. Buying new technologies will also require up-front capital, expense, and time to learn how to use them, with the understanding that these costs will be returned only through future increased profits. Try hard to avoid purchasing technologies simply because they are the latest thing. However, if you have a need and a new technology will fill it, you should not hesitate if it will increase your profits.

Is Outsourcing Right for Your Company?

Before you decide to jump in the pool and start swimming with the outsourcing experts in other companies, you must determine if outsourcing is right for your company. Not every company can handle the myriad aspects of outsourcing, and those that recognize that outsourcing is not right for them save lots of time and money by not going forward with any outsourcing plan.

One factor that might influence a company's decision to outsource is the corporate culture. How is the corporate culture at your business? Do you think it is ready to try—and succeed at—outsourcing? Do you have support from your key management-team members, and are they excited and can't wait to get started? Or are some of your management-team members not quite sure if this is right for them? Watch out for the red flags; they are there. Do not get so caught up in "I will make outsourcing work for our company" that you ignore the warning signs. If you do, they may come back to haunt you sooner than you think.

If your company is considering an outsourcing proposition, keep these five tips in mind:

1. Does your company have projects or departments that are beginning to get too difficult to handle in-house? If so, then outsourcing might be the answer. However, before making the move to outsourcing, make sure that you are not suffering from some internal management problem that can be solved with a few personnel changes.

2. Have you taken an inventory to determine if outsourcing will be cost-effective? In other words, if you are having problems with a department or a division, don't automatically think that outsourcing will make things better. If you

need to, hire an outside consultant to help you determine whether outsourcing is right or you need to restructure.

3. Does your company need to make capital funds available? If so, why? And if so, how much will satisfy your expansion needs? Make sure you do an effective cost study to see if outsourcing will be the answer.

4. Are you looking at outsourcing as a means of cutting costs? If so, tread carefully. The first few years of outsourcing may contain hidden costs that you were not aware of.

5. Are you ready to risk a little? When a company makes the decision to move forward with an outsourcing project, things can, and will, go wrong. There are hundreds of horror stories of companies that have nearly gone bankrupt because they failed to plan accordingly. When you think you have all of your ducks in a row, then go back and examine them a second and even a third time. When you are ready to risk, you want to make sure you have all of your bases covered!

Imperatives

Although modern outsourcing has been developing for some 50 years, there are still problems associated with many outsourced operations. Despite the best of intentions and planning, there will be times when things will go wrong.

It's not always right to outsource; outsourcing doesn't always work. Sometimes outsourcing may have been the right decision, but the process and/or execution were flawed. Staffing.org have identified five imperatives that address the problems associated with outsourcing. Acting on them will optimize your outsourcing performance and eliminate the failures:

1. Organization leaders should focus on objectives, not strategy.
2. More and better performance metrics must be developed.

3. Organizations should approach *all* resourcing decisions holistically.

4. Human resources should assume responsibility for all human capital aspects of outsourcing.

5. Resourcing decision should be based on performance.

Focusing on Objectives, Not Strategy

Our obsession with strategy is sorely misguided. Many executives make the mistake of thinking "If our strategy is clearly determined, nothing can go wrong." That line of thinking has sunk many outsourcing ships.

So many books, speeches, presentations, and consultants are focused on strategy. It's no wonder that the business world has become obsessed with that word. In the Foreword to a popular business book, *The HR Scoreboard*, the authors, Brian E. Becker, Mark A. Huselid, and Dave Ulrich (Harvard Business School Press, 2001), note that they always "start with the same simple question, 'What is your strategy?' "

That should never be the first question. Putting strategy first will produce the same results as ready, fire, aim. The right order is:

Mission.

Objectives.

Strategy.

Strategy has always been third, never first, and the more emphasis put on mission and objectives, the easier it will be to develop the strategy. "If you get the objectives right, a lieutenant can write the strategy" is a statement most often credited to George Marshall. He was an extraordinary military leader and the recognized architect of the Allied victory in World War II. As secretary of state and architect of the rebuilding of Europe, president of the Red Cross, and secretary of defense, Marshall also believed in the importance of objectives. A recipient of the Nobel Peace Prize, George Marshall was undisputedly one of the most effective leaders of the twentieth century.

Although military leaders are responsible for this approach, it isn't just a military thing. I have worked with private and public organizations around the world. They include the elite and the mundane, the large and the small. Invariably, ineffective organizations do not have clear objectives. During an effectiveness engagement in Atlanta, the CEO of a national professional-services firm became ever more exasperated as he heard his nine direct reports articulate nine noticeably different mission statements and struggle with their own departments' objectives. Leaders of the core functions in highly profitable organizations are invariably obsessed with their objectives but have met with vice presidents of functions supporting them who may talk strategy but are not able to articulate their departments' objectives. The surest way to improve any organization's performance is to take the time to get the objectives right. Employees at any level who do not know and understand the purpose of the organization and its objectives will not perform effectively, and they certainly will not be able to make the best decisions about outsourcing or anything else.

Many of us, however, are responsible for executing, and the strategy is rightfully left to us. No significant activity should be initiated without a strategy, but it is impossible to determine an effective one unless it is derived from clear, specific objectives. Here is a simple three-step way to get to the strategy:

1. Verify or define the mission—the main purpose for which an organization exists. The mission should make sense to

management, employees, and customers. Missions are relatively long-term-oriented. For most businesses they should also be valid tomorrow, next month, and for at least a year. If there is some doubt about the mission, then take time to make sure everyone is on the same page.

2. Establish objectives—the specific and measurable deliverables that are essential to fulfilling the mission. Objectives should be customer driven if not jointly established and also clear to management, employees, and customers. Most importantly, objectives must be measurable.

3. Now the optimum strategy—the systematic plan of action to attain specific objectives—can be developed.

Those who have the responsibility for executing must also have the authority to adjust or even change the strategy in response to what they experience as they work toward achieving their objectives. We should also note that a strategy is no more than words unless the execution of the strategy includes the requisite structure, resources, processes and procedures or tactics.

Establishing the right objectives is the first responsibility of leaders. Leave the strategy to those responsible for executing.

Improving Performance Metrics

Sabermetrics. It's a great word. I'm sure a consulting firm would be using the term had not baseball already laid claim to it. Sabermetrics is the search for objective knowledge about baseball using mathematical and statistical analysis. Yes, after a century and a half, new metrics have been developed for this, the most measured of our pastimes.

OUTSOURCING

Performance metrics are also about the search for objective knowledge using mathematical and statistical analyses. Baseball metrics help team management to make the best decisions about players and ultimately optimize the team's performance. Although most organizations are more complex than a baseball team, a primary purpose of performance metrics is the same: to make the best resourcing decisions in order to optimize organizational performance.

There are no baseball metrics for strategy, player management practices, or player engagement. Even before sabermetrics, baseball statistics have always measured performance outcomes or results, as should any organization's performance statistics. Performance metrics should be associated with measurable objectives. You can't—and shouldn't try to—measure strategy or practices or engagement.

You'd think that the baseball stats that we've been using for generations have to be the best, but the data supporting sabermetrics is incredibly compelling. Michael Lewis's *Moneyball: The Art of Winning an Unfair Game* (W.W. Norton, 2003) is a must-read book for anyone involved in business or any aspect of human capital management. It's a compelling story about using these new metrics to build a championship-caliber team in the face of 100 years of accepted scouting practices. In spite of the data, sabermetrics have been slow to gain widespread acceptance. *The Wall Street Journal*'s Carl Bialik reported on July 1, 2003 that "self-interest compels veteran writers and broadcasters to reject the idea that stat heads have a better handle on the game than they do."

In business, it's the consultants and pundits who are struggling to hold on to the most overrated and useless of conventional stats. In spite of saber-sharp data, many insist there must be meaning in the metrics because they have been around for so long. The ratio of HR employees to all employees is a good example. Probably the oldest HR metric, it is based on the premise that comparing the number of HR employees to the number of total employees that they support was an indication of HR efficiency, if not performance. A ratio of 1:100 was considered the standard. Like many common metrics, it may sound logical, but it was flawed from inception. What if two HR organizations had the same 1:100 ratio but:

- One HR organization paid its staff twice as much as the other?
- One had a budget that was more than twice as big as the other?
- One supported demanding physicians and research scientists at a dozen locations around the country, while the other supported office workers in one location?
- One was detested by the rest of the organization and the other was highly valued?

Such are the problems with any head count–based metrics, and yet this ratio is how many organizations manage their HR function—and how HR outsourcing organizations sell their services.

The nature of functions such as manufacturing and distribution fostered the development of meaningful metrics, but that is not the case for HR and human capital intensive–operations indicators and performance. This perspective from a major consultancy (watsonwyatt.com, "Incorporating Human Capital into an Integrated Measurement Approach") indicates how convoluted approaches to measuring human capital indicators and performance have become:

Many organizations have difficulty focusing on the "right" measures. They might measure a factor generally related to financial performance, but it may not be the best one considering the business and strategy. For example, organizations know that employee turnover is related to financial performance; and since turnover data is readily available, a company might choose to measure turnover. But if the company's turnover rate is very low, it most likely does not strongly affect the business performance.

This suggests that a metric is important only if the data it measures is poor, but if a metric is valid, it is always valid, regardless of what the answer is. If turnover was a valid metric and the turnover was very low, it still should be measured. If a team measures batting averages and runs batted in, they do it regardless of whether the results are good or bad.

Incidentally, there are many documented cases of organizations with very low turnover that significantly and adversely affected business performance. Low turnover can be a bad thing. Retaining the wrong employees, fostering complacency, or enabling a culture that drives out change agents and high performers may result in low turnover, but it is deleterious to any organization. Regardless, metrics such as turnover and cost per hire are as meaningless a human capital metric as the won-lost record is for pitchers. Retention—retaining the staff you should keep—and recruiting efficiency are far better HR metrics for organizations to always monitor.

Although it is often difficult to evaluate the impact of outsourcing operations because of the lack of a "before" benchmark, outsourced operations tend to be measured more than those that are kept in-house. This is because after an organization outsources work, it is more apt to ask, "What is it costing us now, and what do we get for our money?" We have documented both efficient and incredibly inefficient outsourced operations. The only consistent difference between the two is that the best performers aggressively measure and report their own performance.

There is need for more and better performance metrics in every category of outsourcing, but the need is particularly great for human capital-intensive operations. Under the auspices of Staffing.org, leading outsourcers, consultancies, academics, professional associations, and end user organizations are working together to establish standard metrics and metrics templates to improve the measurement of human capital–intensive performance. The Metrics Roundtable includes Veritude, Hewitt Associates, Saratoga Institute/PricewaterhouseCoopers, and Watson Wyatt. These organizations are taking a leadership role in developing critical approaches and metrics for all organizations.

Until more and better performance metrics are established, keep in mind that valid metrics should:

- Be limited to no more than four for each outcome or result.
- Make sense to everyone associated with them.
- Be easy to understand and to measure.
- Drive continuous performance improvement.
- Be based on requirements established before initiating work.

They should *not* be:

- Strategic—you can't measure strategy.
- Complex.
- Numerous.
- Exclusive.

Approaching *All* Resourcing Decisions Holistically

We can be sure that when the first people started working together in the Stone Age there were management challenges. Then, as now, leaders were always looking for the solution to their problem du jour. The solutions inevitably addressed one aspect of the work that needed to be done. If it was the right aspect, it worked at least for a time until another problem arose, and so on.

This one-fix-at-a-time approach is fundamentally flawed. Only a holistic approach can properly address the complexity and connectivity of everything associated with organization performance, and such an approach provides the best basis from which to make decisions.

No assignment or project—no work of any kind—should ever be initiated without background and context, an agenda with an associated mission, objectives, and a structure to address and effect change. All of these words are synomous with framework, and a holistic performance framework is essential to attain optimum and sustained success in any complex endeavor.

Frameworks include and integrate every aspect of performance and enable organizations to make optimum decisions, now and for the future. Metrics and benchmarks are much more valuable when associated with frameworks. They also accelerate and improve resource selection and allocation decision making.

Like blueprints used in conventional engineering projects, frameworks help you to evaluate an existing organization as well as design and build organizations from scratch. Performance frameworks explain past and current performance as

38

well as anticipate future performance. The holistic frameworks developed by performancesoft Inc. have measurably helped a wide range of organizations, and HREngineer developed a human capital-oriented Performance Blueprint™ based on almost 30 years of research. More and more consultancies are developing proprietary frameworks. The most effective frameworks include:

- All the factors that drive performance.
- A performance cycle.
- All potential options to accomplish the work.

The factors that drive organization performance can be divided into two categories, fundamental and operational. Fundamental factors are fixed or at least long-term. Examples of fundamental factors include:

- Mission.
- Governance.
- Leadership.
- Capital and resources.
- External realities.
- Culture, dynamics, and environment.
- Influencers.
- Compensation and benefit plans.
- Motivators.
- Career and development opportunities.

OUTSOURCING

Operational factors address how the organization functions on a day-to-day basis. Examples of operational factors include:

- Objectives.
- Approach and strategy.
- Design and structure.
- Infrastructure and systems.
- Policies and processes.
- Knowledge and skills base.
- Expertise.
- Customer dynamics.
- Working groups.
- Change/learning posture.

These are the factors that the answers depend on. As this information is collected, the data will start to clarify the situation and options. The better job you do of addressing these factors, the more reliable your decision will be. This isn't rocket science, but there is a science to it and the associated outcomes are predictable. These factors cover all the bases and will bring to light any small problems that should be addressed until big problems are fixed.

A specific performance cycle may total over 100 steps, but these are the major and most important ones:

- Acquisition.
- Performance.
- Key performance indicators.
- Organization results.

- Assessment.
- Readiness, depth, vulnerability, diversity, succession planning.
- Development.
- Retention.
- Change.

Today there are myriad options to perform any type and category of work ranging from employees to contractors or consultants to completely outsourced operations. If you approach all work design and structure with these five steps, you'll have a sound and continuing basis from which to make the best decisions.

1. **Evaluate the work.**
   - What is the work that needs to be done and what are the associated performance standards?
2. **Determine the span, time, and location.**
   - How long will you need the work?
   - What hours and days should it be operational?
   - What are the location requirements or limitations?
3. **Establish your options.**
   - What are your available and viable human capital options (employees; consultants, contractors, contingent labor; outsourced operations)?
   - What are the available and viable location options?
4. **Compare the performance standards, including costs, associated with each option.**
5. **Rank your options.**

OUTSOURCING

These steps help the organization to understand what is involved in acquiring and managing any service, internal or external.

We shouldn't be accepting simple explanations from consultants, pundits, vendors, each other, or even from our own management. The right initial answer to whether to outsource and where to base operations should be, "It depends," and it should depend on the answer to series of questions such as these:

- What doesn't it tell us and what doesn't it do?
- What problems have been encountered previously?
- Is there any documentation?
- Can I see the calculations?
- How do you know that?
- What other factors are or may be involved?
- What are the possible implications—now and for the long term?
- How do you define _____?
- What are the other alternatives?
- What are the costs after implementation?
- What does it encourage and what does it discourage?
- What is behind the endorsements or recommendations?
- Are there any other considerations?

Before you make a decision whether it is design and structure or outsource or not, ascertain what you are getting for your dollars now. Then examine the drivers of your current performance. A single factor like superior leadership can compensate for a host of weaknesses—but only for a time.

Human Resources' Responsibility for Human Capital Aspects of Outsourcing

One of HR's traditional responsibilities is to ensure that all employees are treated in accordance with organization policy and the laws of the jurisdictions in which the organization operates. The HR department should assume that responsibility for all outsourced operations as well.

Not long before he died, Isaac Asimov told an audience of HR executives that they bore the heavy responsibility for doing what was right for every one of their organization's workers. He went on to say that they could be assured that what was right ultimately made good business sense, so if they didn't do things because they were right, they should do them because they made good business sense. He concluded by saying that if they did not do what was right for their employees or because it made good business sense, they would be forced to do it because of public opinion, the marketplace, or the law, or they would come to regret not doing it.

This is not to suggest that HR revert to the policing role that annoys both management and employees. Human resources has started to embrace measurement of its own performance and document its contributions to organizations. It is also uniquely positioned to help organizations measure and develop all functions of human capital performance.

Even in mature outsourcing markets like manufacturing, IT, and call centers, progressive HR functions can fundamentally improve effectiveness. As customers, we've all experienced outsourced call centers. Staffing.org evaluated four U.S.-based and seven offshore call centers and found that there was a lack of clear HR policies and procedures in the worst-performing ones, and there was definitive and consistent HR leadership in the best.

Sheraton Hotels and Resorts, where customer-service calls may be routed to any of eight locations around the world, is an example of the best. Sheraton's seamless service was the best of all the call centers evaluated. Every representative reached by Staffing.org not only provided exceptional service but also had a great deal of pride in their work and in the organization—including their co-workers in their call center and the other seven centers around the world. They actually bragged about the other locations. Good HR deserves at least some of the credit.

Human resources should be tasked with the responsibility for not just employees, but also for the human capital aspects of outsourced operations. Their expertise should be on call for a manufacturing facility in China, program operations in India, or a call center in Ireland.

The full potential of outsourcing has yet to be tapped. Putting objectives first, establishing good metrics, approaching all resourcing holistically, and giving HR responsibility for all its human capital aspects will help.

Performance-Based Resourcing Decisions

The only proven indicator of a candidate's future performance is that candidate's prior performance in a similar position and venue. Prior performance is also a very good indicator of an outsourcing provider's performance. We should obtain all appropriate performance information before making any important decisions.

Getting accurate performance information on outsourcing providers is, however, difficult. The nature of their sales and the sales cycle of the organization understandably discourages sharing performance information. Confidentiality requirements also preclude making information available, even if the provider is willing to disclose. Outsourcing is by nature competitive. Organizations don't want to publicize failures, and even successes are often proprietary. There is a solution.

New, sophistical buyers' services such as OnPerformance (OnPerformance.com) were established to provide background and performance information to help organizations make better decisions. Based on surveys of corporate executives and ongoing focus groups, OnPerformance was designed to provide organizations with the information they want and need, the way they want it. Its reliability certification has stringent requirements for financial and operational stability and appropriate operating and ethical standards.

OnPerformance also has a secure process by which organizations can confidentially rate and review their outsourcing providers' performance. This process actually drives continuous improvement for the current clients as well as providing important information for potential clients.

Outsourcing is complicated, and a host of reasons drive the success or failure of any outsourced operation. These five imperatives will help to optimize the performance of any outsourced operation.

CHAPTER
4

How Do I Begin Outsourcing?

Why Management, Management, and More Management Are the Keys to a Successful Outsourcing Partnership

The governance process is helped enormously by careful and detailed preparation before the contract is even signed, says John Kopeck, president of Compass North America, who was interviewed for *Outsourcing Essentials*, published by the Outsourcing Institute. "Important, written documentation should be preceded by a thorough understanding of the type of relationship the client wants to achieve over the life of the contract. The amount of time and effort required to

48

structure a deal depends on the type of relationship being built," he says.[1]

Key considerations include:

- *Pricing.* Is the client willing to pay a premium for specialized expertise and business knowledge, or is low cost the primary objective?
- *Vendor involvement.* Does the client expect a high or low degree of input and advice from the outsourcer?
- *Length of relationship.* Does the client seek a long-term relationship, or are frequent vendor changes to be expected?
- *Number of qualified vendors.* Are the services sought by the client highly specialized or widely available?

TOP 10 DRIVERS BEHIND TODAY'S OUTSOURCING DECISIONS

- Acceleration of reengineering benefits.
- Access to world-class capabilities.
- Cash infusion.
- Freeing up resources for other purposes.
- Function difficult to manage or out of control.

---

[1]Emily Leinfuss, "Why Management, Management, and More Management Are the Keys to Successful Outsourcing Partnerships," *Outsourcing Essentials* 2, no. 2 (Summer 2004).

- Improved company focus.
- Making capital funds available.
- Reducing operating costs.
- Reducing risk.
- Resources not available internally.

Acceleration of Reengineering Benefits

Reengineering aims for dramatic improvements in critical measures of performance such as cost, quality, service, and speed. However, the need to increase efficiency can come into direct conflict with the need to invest in the core business. As noncore internal functions are continually put on the back burner, systems become less efficient and less productive. By outsourcing a noncore function to a world class provider, the organization can begin to see the benefits of reengineering.

Access to World-Class Capabilities

World-class providers make extensive investments in technologies, methodologies, and people. They gain expertise by working with many clients facing similar challenges. This combination of specialization and expertise gives clients a competitive advantage and helps them avoid the cost of chasing technology and training. In addition, there are better career opportunities for personnel who move to the outsourcing provider.

Cash Infusion

Outsourcing often involves the transfer of assets from the company to the provider. Equipment, facilities, vehicles, and licenses used in the current operations have value and are sold to the vendor. The vendor then uses these assets to provide services back to the client. Depending on the value of the assets involved, this sale may result in a significant cash payment to the company.

When these assets are sold to the vendor, they are typically sold at book value. The book value can be higher than the market value. In these cases, the difference between the two actually represents a loan from the vendor to the company, which is repaid in the price of the services over the life of the contract.

Freeing Up Resources for Other Purposes

Every organization has limits on the resources available to it. Outsourcing permits an organization to redirect its resources, most often people resources, from noncore activities toward activities that serve the company. The organization can redirect these people or at least the staff slots they represent onto greater value-adding activities. People whose energies are currently focused internally can now be focused externally—on the customer.

Function Difficult to Manage or Out of Control

Outsourcing is certainly one option for addressing this problem. It is critical to remember that outsourcing doesn't mean abdication of management responsibility, nor does it work well as a knee-jerk reaction by a company in trouble.

When a function is viewed as difficult to manage or out of control, the organization needs to examine the underlying causes. If the requirements, expectations, or needed resources are not clearly understood, then outsourcing won't improve the situation; it may in fact exacerbate it. If the organization doesn't understand its own requirements, it won't be able to communicate them to an outside provider.

Improved Company Focus

Outsourcing lets a company focus on its core business by having operational functions assumed by an outside expert. Freed from devoting energy to areas that are not in its expertise, the company can focus its resources on meeting its customers' needs.

Making Capital Funds Available

There is tremendous competition within most organizations for capital funds. Deciding where to invest these funds is one of the most important decisions that senior management makes. It is often hard to justify noncore capital investments when areas more directly related to producing a product or providing a service compete for the same money.

Outsourcing can reduce the need to invest capital funds in non-core business functions. Instead of acquiring the resources through capital expenditures, they are contracted for on an as-used operational expense basis. Outsourcing can also improve certain financial measurements of the firm by eliminating the need to show return on equity from capital investments in noncore areas.

Reducing Operating Costs

Companies that try to do everything themselves may incur vastly higher research, development, marketing, and deployment expenses, all of which are passed on to the customer. An outside provider's lower cost structure, which may be the result of a greater economy of scale or other advantage based on specialization, reduces a company's operating costs and increases its competitive advantage.

Reducing Risk

Tremendous risks are associated with the investments an organization makes. Markets, competition, government regulations, financial conditions, and technologies all change extremely quickly. Keeping up with these changes, especially those in which the next generation requires a significant investment, is very risky.

Outsourcing providers make investments on behalf of many clients, not just one. Shared investment spreads risk, and significantly reduces the risk borne by a single company.

Resources Not Available Internally

Companies outsource because they do not have access to the required resources within the company. Outsourcing is a viable alternative to building the needed capability from the ground up. New organizations, spin-offs, or companies expanding into new geography or new technology should consider the benefits of outsourcing from the very start.

Source: The Outsourcing Institute, www.outsourcing.com.

IS OUTSOURCING A GOOD WAY TO GROW YOUR BUSINESS?

Outsourcing has become a big deal in our economy. There are articles and books written on it all the time, and you can attend countless seminars and speeches on the subject. I just did a Google search on *outsourcing* and got 1,130,000 links. You can find a lot of information on this subject, and a lot of opinions on how to do it right or screw it up!

One popular idea is that you should decide what you are good at and outsource everything else—that is, focus your company on your core competency, and let someone else do the rest. That logic is sound in theory, and to a certain degree in practice, but, like everything else, you can take it too far. The key is to understand your business and its goals and decide how outsourcing might help you attain them.

OUTSOURCING

When thinking about what to outsource, some things (legal services, printing, health insurance, etc.) are fairly obvious, and most companies outsource them. Some functions are a bit less obvious, and some companies outsource them or not depending on their personal expertise. For example, if you have an accounting background, you probably keep your own books and file your own taxes. There are other things that many companies could—but probably shouldn't—do themselves. For example, most people could create a basic Web page or design their own logo, but the differences between doing it yourself and hiring a professional can be significantly evident in the end result.

There are some things that are crucial to your business that you should probably not outsource. You need to keep an eye (your eye!) on them at all times. These include management and, in many cases, customer interaction.

Some tasks make sense to outsource initially and bring in-house later. If, for example, you aren't very experienced at hiring a receptionist, you could turn to a temp agency to hire one for you. They will charge you a premium, but for that you get significant value; they will understand your requirements, advertise for people, screen them, and place them at your site with no risk to you. If they don't work out for whatever reason, you just call the temp agency and tell them to send someone else. When you find the right person and decide you want them for the long term, you can pay the temp agency a fee and make them a regular employee (i.e., transition from outsourced to in-house).

Although this scenario is common, you don't have to view outsourcing as something to do until you have enough work for an employee. One of the big advantages to outsourcing is flexibility—it can be a lot easier to cut back on a vendor than an employee. (Think of how you would feel if you had to tell an employee who is dependent on her job that you need her only half-time now.) Another advantage is that you don't have to become an expert in a particular area. You can depend on the outsourced company to be the expert, as in the earlier example about web site/logo.

Perhaps the most positive thing about outsourcing is its ability to save you money. This will, of course, depend on the size of your company and what specific tasks you outsource, but, in general, if you think it through, you can save money. For example, my company outsources its IT services (help desk, computer support, and maintenance), and we pay significantly less than we'd pay for a full-time IT person to give us the same level of support. We also outsource our office administration, with similar savings. As we grow, we'll continue to reevaluate these decisions. It may be that the business case for the IT outsourcing will remain good as we grow but that we might eventually hire someone to offload other work from our current people, and since we would be paying them anyway, we could get them to do the bookkeeping as well.

A disadvantage to outsourcing is that you are putting part of your company in someone else's hands. You have to ask yourself if you can trust them, if you think they'll stay in business, and if they can adapt to your growing/changing needs.

UNIVERSITY OF MICHIGAN GOES OFFSHORE

The University of Michigan Business School recently opened a new research center in Bangalore, India, it was reported in the summer 2004 issue of *Outsourcing Essentials*.

Scholars at the Center for Global Resource Leverage: India will study managerial issues and emerging practices in leveraging global resources and accessing new markets. Research will focus on the interface between global companies and Indian firms and on the issues and challenges associated with maximizing the talent pool and knowledge infrastructure in India. Areas of study include: services outsourcing, manufacturing outsourcing, the Indian economy, India-U.S. business interaction, and market opportunities at the "bottom of the economic pyramid."

Initially, about a dozen faculty members from the University of Michigan Business School will be affiliated with the center, which will be co-directed by professors C. K. Prahalad and M. S. Krishnan.

"We will focus on next practices, not best practices," said Prahalad, professor of corporate strategy and international business, in a statement. "The center's first priority is to isolate issues of great importance for the future and frame them to create the right debate, both in the business community and in public policy."

Krishnan, professor of business IT, said, "The center will bring research findings into the classroom so that our students have a better understanding of the opportunities and challenges in this global restructuring of industries and can reflect on the specific capabilities needed to thrive as a successful leader in a global economy."

The center also will offer executive education programs in India. Topics include: co-creating unique value with customers, strategic human resource management, and managing in the context of global competition.

Business School dean, Robert Dolan says the center is a perfect fit for the school, which has established deep linkages with India.

Says Dolan: "The center is a response to the emerging pattern of restructuring of industries and the value chains of firms. Increasingly, managers are focusing methods to leverage resources globally. And India presents a promising opportunity to do that."

FIVE THINGS TO REMEMBER WHEN STARTING AN OFFSHORE PROGRAM

Tandy Gold had to learn on the fly about how to put together an offshore outsourcing program when she was hired by FleetBoston Financial Corporation. Here are some of her do's and don'ts:

- Just do it, even if it's politically difficult.
- Don't lock yourself into a single-vendor relationship for more than three years.
- Don't overemphasize knowledge of your applications. Look beyond just U.S.-based outsourcing firms, too. Try to include an Indian one.
- Make sure you set expectations with your management team, especially because the cost-benefit of such a program generally entails a long-term payoff.
- If you can, try to do some HR planning up front. Any workers outplaced by the program should be outplaced gracefully.

Source: Martha Yang, *Outsourcing Essentials*, Fall 2003.

Vertical Integration and Outsourcing Considerations in the Health-Care Sector

S ome of the steps required to produce the good or service are facilitated by contracting with outside parties whereas others are completed by coordinated actions among the firm's various internal resources. Thus, questions arise regarding the manner in which particular firms choose to organize their activities. How do firms decide which transactions to pursue in the market and which to conduct among internal departments? In other words, how do firms determine the appropriate degree of vertical integration of their operations? And is there an optimal solution?

This question has been addressed by a number of academic frameworks and through empirical studies in several industries. This chapter will examine these theories and apply them to the questions of firm organization and outsourcing within the context of the U.S. health-care industry, with a specific focus on outsourcing decisions by hospitals.

Hospitals were chosen as the basic unit of analysis for a number of reasons. Perhaps, most importantly, they have historically demonstrated a high level of vertical integration and the health-care sector continues to lag behind the overall economy in terms of the degree to which it relies on outsourcing. Most hospitals are relatively sizable, and their quasiresidential nature requires them to provide a number of services, such as food service, that lie outside their presumed raison d'être of treating illness. In addition, hospitals are complex organizations that must keep up with technological change and operate within a complex regulatory and insurance environment, creating a tension between the need to remain adaptable while maintaining a large bureaucracy to oversee complex operations. Finally, although financial considerations play a key role, many hospitals are charitable institutions charged with preserving human life, which leads to some interesting ethical and societal questions regarding the decision to outsource certain functions that may not be raised in the context of other industries, such as manufacturing.

This chapter is organized into three sections. The first will provide a review of economic and other literature addressing firm organization and the drivers of outsourcing decisions. The second will provide a brief overview of the hospital sector and highlight some industry-specific considerations. The final section will apply the frameworks laid out in section one to two specific functions that are organized internally at some hospitals and outsourced by others. One of these areas will be radiology, a clinical function directly related to patient care, and the other will be food service, which is an ancillary service offering.

Transaction Cost Analysis

The question of firm organization was addressed by Ronald Coase in a well-known and often-cited article entitled "The Nature of the Firm," which was published in 1937. Coase explored the forces that determine the size and scope of a firm. Pointing out that economists have historically focused on the price mechanism as the main coordinating factor within an economic system, Coase sought to explain why firms, which have an entrepreneur as the key mechanism for coordinating their activities, exist at all.

His conclusion was that there had to be a cost to using price as the key determinant in allocating factors of production. Costs cited by Coase included discovery of what the relevant prices are, structure/negotiation of contracts or conditions for each exchange of goods or services, uncertainty associated with future needs or availability of supply and government regulation such as sales tax, quotas, and price controls.

Coase conceded that organizing activities within the context of the firm was also not costless. Costs are involved in contracting with employees, managing the various activities undertaken by the firm, and determining the most efficient manner in which to deploy the productive resources of the firm. Coase, therefore, determined that "the principle of marginalism works smoothly. The question always is, will it pay to bring an extra exchange transaction under the organising authority?"[1] Recognizing that the costs of coordinating activity within a firm in-

---

[1] R. H. Coase, "The Nature of the Firm," *Economica*, New Series, 4, no. 16 (November 1937), 404.

crease as it grows increasingly complex in size and breadth of activities, Coase posits that an equilibrium point exists at which conducting an activity within the firm will cost the same amount as it would cost another firm to do so or, effectively, the market price of procuring the activity's output from a third party. Coase also pointed out that firms are dynamic in nature, and he claimed that "an investigation of the effect changes have on the cost of organizing within the firm and on marketing costs generally will enable one to explain why firms get larger and smaller . . . [providing] a theory of moving equilibrium."[2] Thus was born the Transaction Cost Analysis (TCA) approach to understanding the make-versus-buy decision.

The ideas of TCA were extended by authors who considered other types of costs that influence a firm's organizational choices. Articulated by Klein, Crawford, and Alchian in 1978 and Williamson in a series of papers beginning in the 1970s, the premise is that the certain difficulties associated with conducting transactions in the open market (market failures) can raise the potential costs to firms, and that, under certain conditions, firms can mitigate these costs by bringing the associated functions in house.

These later authors were more explicitly concerned with governance, viewing spot market transactions, long-term contracts, and vertical integration as simply different ways of governing the same function: ensuring that the firm has access to a desired product or service. As summarized by Joskow (1988), the revised model provides a "fairly specific theory for explaining the structure of vertical relationships based on variations in

---

[2]Ibid., 405.

the importance of asset specificity, uncertainty . . . and the constraints of repeat purchase activity."[3]

The most important concept added to Coase's framework is that of asset specificity or idiosyncratic transactions. Asset specificity refers to the degree to which a factor of production or service capability is customized. The argument runs that, if an asset is highly specific (and critical) to a particular function, then the possibility exists for a supplier to engage in opportunistic behavior and effectively hold its customer hostage. This behavior is motivated by two factors. First, the market for the asset is limited by definition, and, therefore, so, too, is the universe of potential buyers. As a result, the supplier can improve its position only by exacting greater rents from its existing customer(s). Second, few suppliers are likely willing to invest in developing the capabilities required to supply such an asset, particularly if the required capital investment is high. The buyer, therefore, is left with few alternative sources and switching to a new relationship could be costly and disruptive. A rational firm will attempt to deal with these problems at the time it enters a supply contract, but such arrangements are necessarily imperfect. In addition, the more complex the contracts become in order to deal with contingencies, the more expensive they become to negotiate and administer.

Uncertainty about future demand or technology in and of itself does not necessarily spur vertical integration. In fact, a number of theorists have argued that firms facing high degrees of uncertainty, especially uncertainty about technologi-

---

[3]Paul L. Joskow, "Asset Specificity and the Structure of Vertical Relationships: Empirical Evidence," *Journal of Law, Economics, & Organization* 4, no. 1 (Spring 1988), 101.

cal change, may actually hinder their competitiveness if they pursue high degrees of integration.[4] The point made by Williamson and others is that uncertainty is likely to be far more costly if transactions involve a high degree of asset specificity. For nonspecific assets, continuity matters less because presumably many alternate sources of supply exist and switching costs are less significant. It is impossible to conceive and enforce a contract that will take into consideration every eventuality and responses thereto. Therefore, when combined with asset specificity, uncertainty may drive firms to seek greater control by bringing capabilities in house. Doing so is perceived to facilitate specialized decision making, improve communication efficiency, and ensure greater commonality of interests among key players.[5]

Repeat purchase activity or transaction frequency is also an often cited determinant of vertical integration. Its predictive characteristics are also tied to the level of asset specificity. With respect to low-specificity assets, frequency of purchase is unlikely to matter. Because markets are competitive and specialized investments are not required, firms should be able to efficiently source low-specificity assets regardless of the frequency with which they do so. For high-specificity assets, however, frequency is more likely to matter. The implied requirement for highly specialized investment indicates that, for low-frequency items, vertical integration may be suboptimal,

---

[4]Kathryn Rudie Harrigan, "Matching Vertical Integration to Competitive Conditions," *Strategic Management Journal* 7, no. 6 (November–December 1986), 543.

[5]Saul Klein, Gary L. Frazier, and Victor J. Roth, "A Transaction Cost Analysis Model of Channel Integration in International Markets," *Journal of Marketing Research* 27, no. 2 (May 1990), 199.

because the requisite resources are likely to sit idle for long periods of time. When there is high frequency for assets of this type, vertical integration may be more optimal.[6]

In the context of service providers, an interesting opposing view has been raised by Murray and Kotabe (1999). These authors argue that service firms may be better off developing in-house capabilities even for highly idiosyncratic items. Three key factors are cited: (1) the difficulties associated with making an adequate assessment of the capabilities of a third party being selected to provide the services when they are used only infrequently, (2) lack of incentives for suppliers to invest in or excel at these less frequently demanded services and (3) the competitive advantage that may be provided to a firm that distinguishes itself by offering these services and performing them well.[7]

The Capabilities Approach

The importance of company-specific skills from a strategic perspective has been discussed by numerous authors. Known by various names—core competencies, firm-specific competence, invisible assets—these are generally described as firm-specific skills and knowledge that are developed over time within a company. Prahalad and Hamel (1990) conceptualize core competencies as the roots of the corporation, from which core products and business units spring and ultimately bear

---

[6]O. E. Williamson, "Transaction-cost Economics: The Governance of Contractual Relations," *Journal of Law and Economics* 22 (1979), 233–261.

[7]Janet Y. Murray and Masaaki Kotabe, "Sourcing Strategies of U.S. Service Companies: A Modified Transaction Cost Analysis," *Strategic Management Journal* 20, no. 9 (September 1999), 798.

the fruit of end products.[8] Perhaps a more academic definition is provided by Dorothy Leonard-Barton (1990), who views "a core capability as the knowledge set that distinguishes and provides a competitive advantage."[9] Leonard-Barton highlights four dimensions to this knowledge set: (1) employee knowledge and skills, (2) technical systems, (3) managerial systems, and (4) values and norms.

When applied to questions of firm organization, the capabilities approach addresses what has been cited by critics as a shortcoming of the TCA: its failure to address the cost of information in the context of the production process. Under the transaction-cost framework, the make-or-buy decision hinges upon a comparison of transaction costs (if purchasing from a supplier) and management costs (if producing internally), or, as Demsetz (1988) points out, the sum of these costs because internal production will involve some transaction costs and external purchases require some degree of management.[10] The implicit assumption appears to be that what can be produced by one firm can be produced equally well by another, because production costs and skills are not cited as meaningful criteria. The issue of scale economies available to producers that serve a number of customers is presumed to be insignificant, because

---

[8]C. K. Prahalad and Gary Hamel, "The Core Competence of the Corporation," *Harvard Business Review* (May–June 1990), 81.

[9]Dorothy Leonard-Barton, "Core Capabilities and Core Rigidities: A Paradox in Managing New Product Development," *Strategic Management Journal* 13, Special Issue: Strategy Process: Managing Corporate Self-Renewal (Summer 1992), 113.

[10]Harold Demsetz, "The Theory of the Firm Revisited," *Journal of Law, Economics and Organization* 4, no. 1 (Spring 1988), 148.

firms would have the option of producing for their own needs and selling additional supply to outsiders.[11]

The capabilities approach to organizational decisions suggests that production skill does matter. Its core premise is that firms will bring activities in house if their capabilities in these activities are superior to those of a potential supplier. Thus, the degree to which a firm is vertically integrated is a function of the breadth of its capabilities, according to this framework. The basic proposition of the capabilities approach is summarized nicely by Nicholas Argyres: "Firms vertically integrate into those activities in which they have greater production experience and/or organizational skills (i.e. 'capabilities') than potential suppliers and outsource activities in which they have inferior capabilities, . . . all else constant."[12]

Support for this viewpoint emerges from a study conducted by Walker and Weber (1984) on make-versus-buy decisions made within a division of a U.S. automotive company. Drawing heavily from Williamson's framework, the authors looked at the influence of transaction costs on the company's decisions through the effects of competitiveness among suppliers, uncertainty regarding volume, and uncertainty regarding technology. Their results indicated that the effect of production costs was substantially more significant than transaction costs. Both types of uncertainty were found to have a statistically significant effect, but it was much smaller than that of production costs. It is interesting to note that the authors attribute the importance of

---

[11]Nicholas Argyres, "Evidence on the Role of Firm Capabilities in Vertical Integration Decisions," *Strategic Management Journal* 17, no. 2 (February 1996), 130.
[12]Ibid., 131.

production cost in part to the nature of the product. The components being evaluated were relatively simple, suggesting that detailed measurements of fully loaded production costs could be made with relative ease.[13]

A second study performed by Richard Langlois and Paul Robertson (1989) provides additional evidence on the influence of firm capabilities. The authors analyzed vertical integration during the early years of the U.S. automobile industry. They found that early on, the pace of change and innovation was such that manufacturers were forced to integrate aspects of their production process because their suppliers could not keep pace with the rate of change taking place in production methods and model design. As Ford refined its methods of division of labor on the assembly line and mass production, it began to build much of its production equipment internally, even though outside machine-tool shops had been successfully utilized in the past. According to Langlois and Robertson, this occurred because the pace at which Ford engineers were redesigning the production process rendered the toolmakers' capabilities obsolete and only Ford insiders really understood the use to which the new machinery would be put. In addition, the vertical integration was, for a time, self-reinforcing. Because most of the assembly activity took place in one location, Ford engineers were in a far better position than outsiders to observe opportunities for improvement and economies of scale. Over time, as the pace of innovation slowed and outside

---

[13]Gordon Walker and David Weber, "A Transaction Cost Approach to Make-or-Buy Decisions," *Administrative Science Quarterly* 29, no. 3 (September 1984), 373–391.

vendors caught up, the required capabilities diffused through-out the marketplace and outsourcing was again available.[14]

Summary

Both of the frameworks just described have strengths and limitations. Transaction cost analysis has the initial appeal of seeming to base the decision-making process on quantitative factors, but in practice there are some real challenges involved with measurement. It can be difficult to distinguish between costs associated with managing aspects of the internal organization versus a transaction cost. In addition, certain costs, such as those associated with information gathering remain elusive. Although some strategic-type considerations are captured in the extended analysis provided by Williamson, the overall framework is somewhat light on strategic elements such as competitive response and market position. These considerations are captured more fully in the capabilities approach, which also focuses on the internalized skill set of the organization. Thus, using aspects of both frameworks to evaluate organizational structure is likely to provide the most complete picture.

Hospital Sector Background

Having briefly reviewed two of the key theoretical models for explaining vertical integration decisions, we turn to an analysis of

---

[14]Richard N. Langlois and Paul L. Robinson, "Explaining Vertical Integration: Lessons from the American Automobile Industry," *Journal of Economic History* 49, no. 2, The Tasks of Economic History (June 1989), 366–367.

specific functional areas of hospitals. We evaluate whether the frameworks described earlier suggest that these are attractive areas for outsourcing or if a hospital is likely to be better served by maintaining or establishing in-house capabilities. A brief overview of current conditions in the hospital sector is first provided.

Outsourcing Trends

Hospitals are fertile ground for investigating questions of vertical integration because they have actually been long-time practitioners of outsourcing, but they lag behind general industry in terms of the degree to which outsourcing has permeated most hospital organizations. In the context of this section, outsourcing refers specifically to services either directly or indirectly related to patient care and hospital administration. Sourcing of manufactured goods, supplies, and the like is considered ordinary in the course of their business and not included.

Historically, outsourced functions have included only perceived noncore services such as food service, housekeeping, and security. Outsourcing statistics for hospitals are somewhat limited, but *Modern Healthcare* estimates that three-quarters of all hospitals outsource at least one function. According to the American Hospital Association, the nation's 4,927 community hospitals incurred about $416.6 billion in expenses in 2002.[15] According to a comprehensive study of Veterans' Hospital Administration (VHA), a hospital co-operative, of its members,

---

[15]*Source:* Community hospitals include all nonfederal, short-term general and specialized hospitals whose services and facilities are made available to the general public.

externally sourced services accounted for approximately 16 percent of their annual budgets.[16] These statistics suggest that expenditures for outsourced services represent approximately $66.7 billion annually. This compares to a rate of approximately 33 percent for general industry, according to VHA.

Table 5.1 presents the top-20 functions outsourced by hospitals in 2002 and 2003, according to a 2004 survey of community hospitals conducted by *Modern Healthcare* magazine. As the table indicates, outsourcing within these 20 categories increased significantly over the measurement period. It is also interesting to note that of the 20 areas listed, one-half can be classified as directly relating to patient care (clinical). These range from specialized functions, such as wound care, to management and staffing of entire departments, like the emergency room. The other half consists of ancillary services that are required to support the institutions but are not directly related to providing medical care to patients, such as food-service operations and grounds keeping.

Industry Trends

The health-care sector is a key force within the U.S. economy, representing approximately 15 percent of total gross domestic product.[17] Spending on hospital care is the single largest category, representing approximately $0.33 of each health-care

---

[16]Cited in Michael Romano, "Outsourcing Everything," *Modern Healthcare* 43, issue 14 (April 5, 2004), 25.

[17]Center for Medicare and Medicaid Services, Office of the Actuary.

Table 5.1   Top 20 Functions Outsourced by Hospitals

Functional Area	Hospital Clients in 2002	Hospital Clients in 2003	% Change
Houskeeping	1,043	1,156	10.8%
Food service	1,084	1,149	6.0%
Laundry	728	1,041	43.0%
Emergency	729	945	29.6%
Clinical/Diagnostic equipment maintenance	269	304	13.0%
Pharmacy	185	217	17.3%
Psychiatric	173	177	2.3%
Wound care	155	175	12.9%
Facility operations/Equipment maintenace	177	172	−2.8%
Security	145	160	10.3%
Parking garage	135	135	0.0%
Physical therapy	37	93	151.4%
Radiology	98	93	−5.1%
Rehabilitation	63	85	34.9%
Urgent care/Primary care	62	72	16.1%
Billing/Collections	47	52	10.6%
Facility grounds	40	42	5.0%
Information systems	29	38	31.0%
Nursing	28	26	−7.1%
Surgery	14	20	42.9%
Total	**5,241**	**6,152**	**17.4%**

Source: Modern Healthcare Magazine, 26th Annual Outsourcing Survey, 9/27/04.

dollar spent.[18] Over the past several years, the sector has faced significant financial pressure from both government payment sources and private payees, principally insurance companies. According to the American Hospital Association, approximately one-third of hospitals had negative overall margins. Facing this unfavorable revenue environment, hospitals have sought ways in which to rationalize costs through strategic initiatives such as consolidation and outsourcing.

Special Considerations

In considering the overall climate in which outsourcing decisions are being made by administrators in the hospital sector, some nonfinancial considerations bear mentioning. Of the nearly 5,000 U.S. community hospitals, approximately 60 percent are not-for-profit institutions. Although this moniker generally refers to an institution's tax status and not its requirement for financial viability, it is nonetheless a significant factor to consider. Because so many hospitals are still technically charitable institutions, the mindset among administrators has historically tended to be more "mission-oriented" than that observed among executives in other industries, broadly speaking. The core mission of a hospital is to treat illness and disease, not necessarily to maximize profit. In addition, people tend to evaluate hospitals based upon patient outcomes rather than financial performance or the price of services.

This backdrop has some interesting implications when discussing outsourcing opportunities. For instance, hospital ad-

---

[18]Ibid.

ministrators interviewed about their outsourcing decisions were extremely concerned with preserving employment. Almost every article on the topic mentioned that numerous employees were either hired by the outsourcing firm or reassigned to other positions in the hospital. Because many of a hospital's functions need to be performed on site even if administered by an outside firm, there may actually be lower friction costs, such as severance, unemployment, and retraining costs, associated with outsourcing by hospitals versus other types of companies in which the function may be redeployed to a remote location. It may, however, also suggest that hospitals have a deeper sense of mission that prevents them from fully rationalizing head count and reaping the potential cost savings available to them.

Figure 5.1 demonstrates that hospital employment has

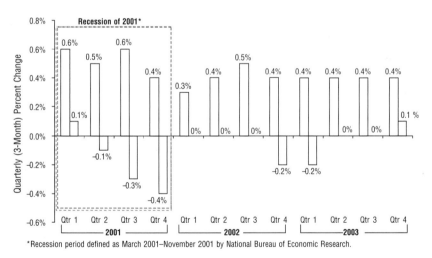

*Recession period defined as March 2001–November 2001 by National Bureau of Economic Research.

Figure 5.1 Percent Change in Employment, Seasonally Adjusted: Hospital vs. All Industries 2001–2003
Source: Department of Labor, Bureau of Labor Statistics.

remained quite stable over the past several years. This is interesting to note because it has already been established that operating profit was generally declining for hospitals and the degree of outsourcing was on the rise during this period. Note that a recessionary environment would not be expected to have a first-order effect on hospitals, because people do not time illness to economic cycles, but it likely did have some impact in the form of lower collection rates, increased pressure from insurance companies, and lower/slower government reimbursement due to the budget deficits observed during this period.

These factors may offer some explanation for why the degree of outsourcing among hospitals has lagged behind that observed in companies of other types. It does not, however, seem to suggest that there is something intrinsically different about the hospital environment that should affect the manner in which such decisions are made. The fact that there may be higher stakes (human life) involved in the process carried out by a hospital can be dealt with within the context of the firm-organizing frameworks as effectively as another type of cost. The monitoring and/or information costs associated with gaining assurances about the capabilities of a provider, and tracking ongoing results of an outsourced program, may be higher in a hospital setting, but these would be factored in to the total cost equation. As long as it can be established that the same standard of care/service will be continued, there does not appear to be a particularly thorny ethical issue with utilizing skilled providers who just happen to work for a firm other than the hospital itself. Employee layoffs can also be handled in the context of costs. To the extent that hospitals value maintaining their employee base highly, then both the tangible and intangible costs of laying off employees would need to be considered in the overall analysis.

We can therefore analyze outsourcing decisions using the vertical integration frameworks laid out in section one.

Case Studies

Two specific functional areas of hospitals will now be evaluated in the context of the models discussed above: overnight radiology coverage and food service. These areas were chosen because they have been outsourced by some hospitals and have remained integrated at others. In addition, they represent both clinical and nonclinical services provided by the hospital.

Food Service

Specialized food-service firms like Aramark and Sodexho USA have been managing the catering operations of hospitals for years, but their penetration remains fairly limited. Industry players disagree about the exact market share held by outsourcing firms, but a range of 20 percent to 30 percent seems reasonable, based on estimates by both hospital associations and outsourcing-firm spokespeople.

Applying the vertical integration frameworks to the food-service function suggests that it is a viable outsourcing candidate. A TCA is somewhat difficult because the actual costs will vary significantly, based upon the size of the hospital and whether it is affiliated with a larger network. Generally, outsourced providers are estimated to provide cost savings of 5 percent to 15 percent because of economies of scale in both purchasing and management. Anecdotal evidence also suggests that they are able to boost food-service revenue as a result of franchise relationships with well-known restaurant brands that can be added to the food courts increasingly found in hospitals, thereby tapping employees and visitors as additional customers for the hospital's food offerings. Such relationships are generally governed by a contract for a fixed period of time, so some amount of management costs will be incurred to negotiate these arrangements and monitor performance.

Internal management of food-service operations does not appear to be significantly burdensome. Administration costs for food-service departments tend to average about 3 percent of a hospital's overall budget. Costs are typically worked into patient billing, and most food-service departments are break-even operations. Thus, the high-level cost analysis does not provide definitive insight into whether food service is an activity best organized internally.

The specificity of assets involved with this function appears unambiguously low. In 2003, approximately 8 million people were employed in restaurants, suggesting that there is a fairly wide pool of potential workers.[19] In addition, the customers of a hospital's food-service department is a captive audience, so the reputation of a particular chef is not likely to create the hold-up problem it potentially would for a restaurant owner, for example. Although there may be some switching costs associated with moving from one outside provider to another, the fact that production takes place on site at the hospital mitigates this cost because access to the fixed assets necessary to run the

---

[19]Department of Labor, Bureau of Labor Statistics, Current Employment Statistics Survey.

department likely could not be impeded by a disgruntled ex-supplier. The limited asset specificity points to outsourcing as a potentially good option. Uncertainty is also quite low, and transaction frequency is quite high. Although the daily census or stream of visitors may vary, it will likely do so within a fairly narrow band that can be estimated based upon historical trends. A baseline level of demand for at least three meals a day is well-assured. Both of these dimensions support the proposition that vertical integration of the food-service function may not be optimal.

From a capabilities perspective, there does not appear to be any compelling reason why a hospital should be better at providing meal service than a firm that focuses specifically on this function. The function also appears to be only tangential to the institution's presumed core competence of patient care. Although there is likely a minimum nutritional standard below which recovery may be impeded, generally speaking, the effect of meals on patient care is weak.

However, a strong food-service department may be a source of competitive advantage because it influences patient satisfaction. Patients have the ability to assess the quality of meals in a very concrete way, which is not necessarily the case for many other aspects of their stay in the hospital. It is difficult for someone to evaluate the skill of their anesthesiologist relative to one at a competing hospital, but they will clearly know if the food is unsatisfactory. That said, there is no real evidence to suggest that an in-house department will do a better job than an outside firm. Therefore, this advantage can be gained just as easily by choosing the best supplier as by maintaining in-house capabilities. Thus, food-service appears to be a viable outsourcing candidate under all aspects of the organizing frameworks.

Radiology

Domestic hospitals have been increasingly turning to outsourcing as a potential solution to a current shortage in U.S. radiologists. Radiology represents one of the few clinical functions that can actually be outsourced to overseas providers. Over the past two years, the typical U.S. radiology department has had an average of four vacancies. This supply problem has exacerbated the existing challenges of having doctors available to read scans taken overnight. Radiologists are often required to work shifts of 24 hours or more, resulting in fatigue, which can have a detrimental effect on performance.

In order to address these problems, a number of offshore radiology practices serving U.S. hospitals have been established in places such as Australia, Israel, and India. In a practice known as *night-hawking*, technological advances have made it possible for X-rays and other scans to be electronically transmitted and interpreted by the overseas physicians in a timely manner, reducing the need to have local radiologists staffing the hospital overnight.

Evaluating this practice purely on cost suggests that hospitals would likely be better off keeping this function in house. Actual transaction costs appear to be fairly neutral. Most overseas practitioners working within this system receive compensation that is roughly equivalent to that of a U.S. radiologist. In addition, there are some additional organizational costs that a hospital incurs by choosing to utilize this system. It is more difficult to ensure quality control when results are being interpreted by doctors thousands of miles away, so most hospitals utilizing these services have policies that require local doctors to review the results a second time in the morning, resulting in some duplicative costs.

However, when some of the other market factors are considered, outsourcing some radiology functions appears to make sense. The question of asset specificity is an interesting one. Radiologists are, to some degree, a specialized asset. Once trained in a specialty, a physician cannot easily switch to a different one without acquiring different skills and training. Additionally, hospitals cannot easily substitute another type of asset, such as an oncologist, for a radiologist. Still, individual radiologists are fairly fungible. Most hospitals require the same general skills held by most by practitioners. Because the assets in this example are employees at will who could leave at any time, the supplier hold-up problem is not eliminated by hiring staff radiologists. Leverage will remain on the side of the practitioner as long as the supply imbalance persists.

Paradoxically, by contracting with a night-hawking firm, the hospital is likely assured of more consistent access to the radiology asset than it would be by trying to maintain full staffing levels in an internal department. The supply problem does not appear to be a significant issue overseas, and there are actually a number of competing firms providing the service. Because the skills among radiologists presumably do not vary significantly, switching costs as a result of contracting with an alternative night-hawk firm or the effects of turnover within a night-hawk's overseas employee base are unlikely to impose significant costs on a hospital.

Uncertainty is fairly high, both in the supply and demand dimensions. On any given evening, the need for radiology services can vary widely. Utilization of in-house assets could be very low or the on-call physician may be quite busy. Because the physician is not paid per scan, efficiency suggests that a minimum number must be read (and billed to patients) each evening in order to absorb the fixed cost of the radiologist's salary. However, the responsibility of the firm to provide the requisite care to patients suggests that it is imperative for it to retain these capabilities at all times despite spotty demand. Perhaps more importantly, there is extreme uncertainty on the supply side. As discussed earlier, the shortage of radiologists effectively creates a hold-up problem that is not eliminated by maintaining an in-house staff.

The radiology function also raises some interesting questions in the context of the capabilities approach. Is there a competitive advantage, defined in this context as superior patient outcomes/satisfaction engendered by internal overnight radiology capabilities? The answer appears to be no. The radiologist is typically a behind-the-scenes player, interacting more frequently in a hospital setting with other physicians than directly with patients. In fact, in many cases, even hospital-employed radiologists or domestic radiological practices will read scans remotely. This suggests that although radiology capabilities are a prerequisite to maintaining a full-service hospital, there is no intrinsic competitive advantage to having someone on site, because technology has eliminated the temporal costs of off-site evaluation. The capabilities framework thus also supports the proposition that vertical integration of radiology functions may not be the optimal strategy for today's hospitals.

Conclusion

Although there is a seemingly endless stream of case studies on other functional areas that could be performed, the foregoing analysis provides insight in two key respects. For one, it suggests that traditional economic frameworks of firm organizational decision making can be applied within the health-care field. As the second section highlights, there are some unique considerations in the hospital sector, but these are really just an idiosyncratic set of market conditions that will impose additional or varying costs. Although perhaps difficult to measure, these costs can nonetheless be factored into the decision-making process and dealt with effectively in the context of both TCA and the capabilities approach.

Secondly, this brief analysis supports the proposition that vertical integration is not necessarily optimal, even for functional areas that are directly related to patient treatment and diagnosis. The radiology example suggests that outsourcing the overnight diagnostic care may actually improve outcomes, because it reduces the stress on hospital-employed radiologists and may lead to fewer errors. In other words, an administrator's default assumption should not be that patient outcomes will be maximized though vertical integration. Rather, a careful evaluation of the cost and capability dynamics of each functional area should be examined in order to facilitate effective decision making about the vertical integration versus outsourcing decisions undertaken by hospitals today.

From the Experts: Life After Outsourcing— A Sourcing Management Model (Outsourcing Is Really Sourcing)

Two-thirds of companies that engage in outsourcing report that their initiatives failed to meet all their intended outcomes, according to Forrester Research.[1] This daunting statistic could intimidate companies from even pursuing outsourcing, but it does not have to. There are ways to ensure you achieve the goals you set for your outsourcing relationships, and this chapter describes one: the Sourcing Management Model.

The Concours Group, a consulting, executive education, and research firm based in Houston, Texas, recently completed an intensive research project, titled Life After Outsourcing (Project LAO), and the Sourcing Management Model was a product of that research. Concours learned that companies getting into

---

[1]Forrester Research, September 2003.

outsourcing often focus too much on the transaction, or the deal itself, and too little on developing a sound strategy and execution plan, which, in every case, means successfully managing the relationship.

When examining relationship management in postoutsourcing environments, Concours found a startling consistency among experienced outsourcing companies about how they handled key outsourcing issues. Their principal mistakes included:

- *Inadequate attention to governance.* Decision rights between the parties need to be clear and consistent, but are often murky and inconsistent. If the authority for decision making is not clear, individuals often don't know which decisions they can and cannot make. The uncertainty around decision making hinders flexibility and communications, resulting in poor or inconsistent execution.

- *A narrow perspective on the relationship.* Outsourcing buyers too often regard outsourcing as simply a contract rather than a mutually beneficial relationship. Changing this mind-set involves, among other things, developing a level of trust between the vendor and purchaser.

- *Failure to set internal expectations.* Internal customers often lack a clear understanding of what the outsourcing partner is able or authorized by the contract to deliver, which frustrates or confuses them. They need to understand the advantages and constraints of the outsourcing arrangement.

- *Lack of process management.* Quite often, neither partner behaves consistently when it comes to managing the activities in the relationship. Both sides must be able to anticipate the behavior of the other in most situations, so it needs to be made predictable. This, again, goes back to trust.

The Sourcing Management Model

With the help of Project LAO members as well as nonmember companies, all of which were large enterprises (annual revenues of $1 billion to $80 billion per year), Concours was able to build a best-practice model that addresses the management of out-sourced activity (see Figure 6.1). (Note: In this chapter we use *sourcing* and *outsourcing* interchangeably.)

These companies collaborated with subject-matter experts to develop a useful tool to manage outsourcing in the steady state. The model will allow companies to translate their strategies into sound outsourcing decision making, followed by execution

Figure 6.1   The Sourcing Management Model

across four key areas: partner relationship management, sourcing program management, sourcing operations management, and service consumer relationship management. It brings the many disciplines, processes, and skills required for a successful life after outsourcing, in which the benefits of outsourcing are fully captured. In short, it makes the various pieces of managing an outsourced environment fit together for a sum greater than its parts.

You can use the Sourcing Management Model two ways. If your company is already engaged in outsourcing, it is a diagnostic tool: Which of these pieces do I already have in place? Which do I have to get better at? Which do I not have at all? Using the model to answer these questions may well reveal solutions to some problem areas that either you are aware of but unable to solve or you were not aware of but can now proactively mitigate.

The second use of the model applies to companies at the beginning of their outsourcing journey. Those companies have not managed large outsourcing arrangements and can learn from the collective experience and best practices of other companies further down the outsourcing path.

The Sourcing Management Model can be applied, not just to outsourcing, but to many kinds of labor sourcing: traditional onshore outsourcing, offshore outsourcing, out-tasking, co-sourcing, and even remotely located insourcing. It reflects the combination and integration of the practices and processes that have led to successful life after outsourcing. Given that no amount of sound management practices can compensate for either the lack of a well-crafted sourcing strategy or an outsourcer's inability to deliver, the Sourcing Management Model can nevertheless ensure that the strategic intents and outcomes of both parties in the outsourcing relationships are achieved—

or to put it another way, that the results expected are the results realized.

Just as important as having a robust Sourcing Management Model is the implementation of a core competency in managing this type of relationship. Companies that focus on building that core competency can leverage the power of specialization, globalization, and virtualization to their advantage, ultimately delivering stronger results for their shareholders and creating a difficult-to-imitate capability that positions them ahead of competitors.

Using the Model

In the following sections, each component of the model is described in detail. It is important to remember that the model works when all of the pieces—strategy, governance, supply management, program management, operations management, and demand management—fit together. It does little good to drive highly effective governance without the framework to implement the decisions. You can develop best-in-class supply management processes and techniques and still fail to achieve the business outcomes if you also do not manage the demand effectively. The model is an integration mechanism, based on the very best practices of experienced companies and practitioners, but it will accomplish little if implemented only in part.

Outsourcing Strategy

"So why was it we decided to outsource IT, anyway?" was the genuine question of a business unit president frustrated with new constraints

resulting from outsourcing most of his corporation's IT function. Whether the decision was right or wrong, nobody should ever have to ask why it was made. This company had clearly done a poor job of explaining its desired outcomes to its own leaders, and would end up paying the price during that difficult first year of outsourcing activity.

Sourcing management strategy must articulate measurable business outcomes that are derived from the overall corporate strategy. Although this chapter focuses on the steady state to outsourcing, long after the strategy is defined, it is important to view it as an ongoing component of sourcing management, informing and influencing the operations. Most companies outsource for some combination of cost savings, strategic or operational focus, flexibility, and innovation. After clearly defining what success looks like in one or more of these four dimensions (see Figure 6.2), companies then make decisions about

- 25% savings over baseline
- Convert $50MM in fixed costs to variable costs
- Reduce capital expenditures by 10%
- Grow EBITDA 10% with fixed operating costs

Cost

- Redeploy 25% of staff to high-value added activities
- Achieve top quartile performance for industry in all back-office processes
- Improve internal customer satisfaction levels by 50%

Focus

- Create ability to ramp up to 25% of resources up or down without layoffs or permanent hires
- Move process execution closer to Asian growth markets

Flexibility

- Combine capabilities of outsourcer and our company for an improved customer experience
- Improve service levels with zero capital expenditure
- Cut software development life cycle by 50%

Innovation

Figure 6.2   Examples of Measurable Business Outcomes

which processes or functions are suitable for outsourcing, what kind of relationship best fits their needs, which provider(s) to select based on the desired relationship, and which locations are acceptable.

Key elements of a sound outsourcing strategy include:

- *A clear exit strategy.* Companies should be prepared to adapt to early, unexpected exits as well as planned ones. There should be a low-risk alternative plan for reintegrating the services into the company if the company chooses that course at the end of the contract. For example, many companies that moved business services to Eastern Europe were caught off guard when labor rates there skyrocketed. The assumption that cost would stay fixed was obviously flawed, but more importantly many lacked a plan exiting their existing contracts that no longer offered the benefits originally expected. Similarly, in the rare cases when a provider proves incompetent at executing the services it is charged with, companies need a relatively painless way to switch providers or bring the outsourced services back in-house.

- *Detailed scenario planning.* This is essential for potential adjustments to the relationship or the services provided, given certain eventualities (e.g., mergers and acquisitions activity, market shifts, strategic changes of direction, and sociopolitical unrest). For example, if your company's growth engine is in China, you might develop scenarios that have you moving your offshore outsourcing activity from India to China over time, in order to apply local skills, language, and political and regulatory expertise to local problems. Another scenario you may consider is the possibility of protectionist legislation being passed in the developed world that would render your existing relationships unprofitable or, worse yet, illegal.

- *A clear set of core values.* These must be upheld by all participants in the relationship. For example, manufacturing and utilities companies pride themselves on safety records. It would send the wrong message to many different constituencies if their chosen outsourcers routinely violated their high standards of safety. Many firms value diversity, and their strategy must include working with providers that do the same.

Outsourcing Governance

A recent conversation between a consultant and three executives (of the same company):

Consultant: *"What does outsourcing governance mean to you?"*
Business Unit President: *"I've always thought of it as centralization."*
Chief Operating Officer: *"It's the retained staff we need to keep around in order to keep the outsourcer from taking advantage of us."*
Global Chief Information Officer: *"I sort of agree. I think we need a new organization to manage our outsourcing deals."*

Governance is the Achilles' heel of outsourcing activity. In fact, many companies that have had an otherwise successful outsourcing experience remarked during Project LAO that they thought they could still improve in this area. Most often, the problem starts with defining what governance is and is not.

Governance specifies what types of decisions need to be made, who is in charge of making them (always in support of the business outcomes), and how these decisions create desired behaviors that lead to the achievement of the business outcomes.

WHY IS OUTSOURCING GOVERNANCE SO DIFFICULT?

Most companies report struggling in some way with governance of their outsourcing initiatives. In the research project, Life After Outsourcing, conducted in late 2004 and early 2005 by the Concours Group, some reasons for this difficulty surfaced.

Misunderstanding of the definition of governance. Perhaps because the current wave of outsourcing and the recent wave of accounting scandals occurred concurrently, *governance* became a hot buzzword that suddenly applied to everything. A rush to govern everything clouded the true meaning and application of governance, leaving companies with half-developed governance models. Governance is the framework of decision rights that encourages desired behaviors in both the outsourcer and the client company. Different companies have used the term interchangeably with "sourcing management organization," "vendor management," and "retained staff," but, in reality, governance is none of these.

Governance and management are different disciplines. Although the former deals with making sound decisions only, the latter deals with making decisions *and* executing a set of processes or activities. Most companies run into trouble when they confuse the two, focusing on the execution at the expense of the truly important, strategic decision making. Execution is still important, but it is not governance.

Counterintuitive behaviors. Because governance deals with decision making, it often requires executives to engage in tough conversations about power—wielding it, sharing it, abdicating it in favor of the corporation's business outcomes. Most companies are not good at specifying who exactly is accountable for a decision, who gets to provide input or recommendations, and who is simply informed after the fact. These are often tense and unpleasant conversations.

Outsourcing further complicates things because it requires the counterintuitive step of *sharing* decision-making power with an outside provider, but any company that has tried to make operational decisions on behalf of its outsourcer has learned the hard way that this leads to contentious relationships, dismal service levels, and poor financial performance of the outsourcing arrangement. When you live in an outsourced environment, you must trust your provider with at least some level of decision making.

Standardization versus customization. The final common challenge about outsourcing governance involves a trade-off between standardization and customization. Many companies have laid out clear cost targets and understood, at least during negotiation of the deal, that the path toward those savings is through consolidation of processes and systems, driving more common, standard solutions across business units. However, when the time comes to make decisions about shared platforms and standards, they allow individual business units to continue making decisions that drive away from these outcomes rather than toward it. The inevitable conclusion seems to be "Outsourcing didn't work," when in fact it is governance that has failed.

OUTSOURCING

How can you test for effective outsourcing governance within your organization? Ask and answer the following questions:

ARE THERE EFFECTIVE OPERATING PRINCIPLES IN PLACE?

Operating principles are a few succinct statements about "the way we work here." Good operating principles focus on the difficult issues, not the easy ones. A strong test of whether an operating principle is sound is whether a rational person could argue the opposite. For example, "We will extract the maximum value from our outsourcing initiatives" is not a good operating principle; clearly no one would argue the opposite. "We will make outsourcing decisions for the benefit of the enterprise first, and the business units second" is better; although this is a perfectly sound principle, there are also any number of business unit presidents who could argue, persuasively, that the opposite should be a guiding principle. A principle, then, is not a reflection of what you believe is right or wrong, but instead a clear articulation of a position you have taken and expect everyone to follow. All good principles link back to strategic intents, drive behavior, are enforceable, and have clear consequences associated with breaking them. You should set up decision-making groups to work together at articulating the operating principles for outsourcing, because the experience of gaining alignment (getting the touchy issues on the table in front of the group that needs to address them) is just as valuable as being able to communicate it to employees and outsourcers. The list that follows is an example of one company's outsourcing operating principles.

Examples of Sound Outsourcing Operating Principles

- We will value and reward partners that invest in the achievement of our business goals.
- We will work as "badgeless" teams all the time, every time.
- We will expect year-over-year performance improvements in cost and quality.
- We will be proactive, tolerant, and encouraging in incorporating the diversity of our partners.
- We will ensure our partners have the opportunity to make a fair profit.
- We will expect to be a Tier 1 customer to all our selected partners.
- We will promote flexibility over cost when the choice presents itself.

ARE THE APPROPRIATE GOVERNANCE BODIES IN PLACE?

Governance bodies, or councils, are groups of individuals that make decisions about outsourcing. An effective outsourcing governance body has a clear charter and resists stepping outside its boundaries. Governance bodies meet at regular intervals and discuss, given predetermined rules of engagement, important decisions around outsourcing. Like any decision-making body, governance councils are most effective when all members understand the strategy (a shared common ground), and when the membership is kept to a minimum. Remember, the goal is to *make* decisions, and it is easier for seven people to make decisions than a dozen. The trick is to balance appropriate representation while keeping the number of decision makers to a minimum.

You should avoid creating new councils specifically for the purpose of outsourcing the decision making. It is always preferable to leverage an existing body by simply adding outsourcing decisions to its scope than to create a carbon copy of the group to make the outsourcing-related decisions.

Membership in outsourcing governance bodies can be rotated, which helps by expanding representation and managing the size of the group. Occasionally, changes in business conditions or specific decisions before the councils will require changes (either permanent or temporary, either additions or deletions) to the membership.

One often overlooked responsibility of a governing council is to define *how* decisions will be made: By majority vote? consensus? Will some votes count more than others? Outsourcing tends to surface the deepest passions of individuals, and clarifying the decision-making process for the group will save many wasteful and potentially bitter discussions.

When providers are represented in these councils, this is a clear sign of strong governance. Typically, more than one governance body is required, not only to drive decisions to the appropriate expertise level, but also to avoid running every decision up to the highest level of executive decision making.

HAVE APPROPRIATE GOVERNANCE DOMAINS BEEN DEFINED?

A domain is one type of decision that must be made in the course of outsourcing. Typical governance domains may include outsourcing strategy (creating or adjusting the strategy itself); service delivery (setting parameters around acceptable service performance); financial management (acting upon positive or negative financial performance of the outsourcing relationship); contract management (approving new contracts or amendments to existing contracts); and communications (approval of what gets communicated to whom and when).

A common pitfall is to assume that the domain and the responsibility for its execution are the same; they are not. For example, if a given outsourcing governance council is asked to make a contract amendment decision, it is not expected to actually execute the amendment, but simply to define what it will say.

It is tempting to define many domains, but to be effective, all decisions should be grouped into no more than five or six domain families. It is easy for companies and their outsourcers to wind up paralyzed over relatively insignificant operational decisions if all decisions must be made at the governance level. In some cases, the number of governance bodies rises in proportion to the number of governance domains, but it is inevitably dysfunctional to have a dozen or more outsourcing decision-making groups.

DO YOU HAVE A DECISION RIGHTS MATRIX?

Governance is about decision making and operating principles are about translating strategy into operating maxims; governance bodies make decisions, and governance domains describe which decisions need to be made. It is the decision-rights matrix that brings all of these together.

In a decision-rights matrix, companies specify exactly which body gets to decide, propose, or influence a decision, based on the operating principles agreed to by all parties. Not all bodies

	Governance Domains				
Governance Bodies	**Strategy**	**Contract**	**Service Delivery**	**Performance Management**	**Communi-cation**
Executive Management	D			I	
Outsourcing Strategy Council	R	I		D	D
Outsourcing Operations Council	I	D	D	R	R
Provider	I	R	R	R	R

R: Recommends D: Decides I: Informed

Key

Figure 6.3 Decision Rights Matrix

need to have specific decision rights for all domains. In Figure 6.3, the company recognized that executive management did not need or want to be informed of every decision, and, instead, entrusted its delegates with some of the important governance domains. The company also wanted to promote managing outcomes, not services, and thus gave ultimate decision rights on service delivery to the provider, retaining the rights to decisions about financial and performance management.

Supply Management

"I know how these people [outsourcers] work: Once they get inside they are going to tell us they can't do what we asked them to do, ask us for more money, and keep telling us we have to change the contract."
        —*A senior executive with no previous outsourcing experience*

Attitudes like this are not uncommon. Suddenly everyone in your company is an expert on outsourcing, and their expertise is generally applied to telling you why outsourcing could never work. In fact, many companies are having great success with outsourcing. One of the ways they calm the waters in the boardroom and build the trust of the organization is by demonstrating outstanding supply management practices.

Many companies say, "We outsource only commodity services." It makes them feel good to know that they are focusing on the more strategic activity within the enterprise. However, that statement also ignores the fact that they are dealing with human talent, and that vendors are now delivering services that just a few years ago the companies were very willing to pay their own employees good money to perform.

The many outsourcing disaster stories serve as reminders that just because a specific skill is broadly available does not mean that you can substitute one set of people with that skill for another at a lower cost and expect the same performance. In the 1990s, several countries in Eastern Europe became popular outsourcing destinations. Initially the labor was inexpensive, and the people were well educated and eager to work for foreign companies. However, most of those countries have small populations and, therefore, a limited pool of qualified talent. Inevitably their overall economic circumstances changed: Their middle classes grew rapidly, their currency strengthened against the dollar and other Western currencies, the individuals working in those centers became more and more skilled in both the functional expertise and the language of their clients, and many received offers to work outside their home country, while others started their own businesses with their savings. Still others moved up to more senior ranks within their companies with no juniors to fill their old jobs. Suddenly the accountant or developer who had been viewed as commodity labor just a year earlier became a highly sought after, very well paid member of the workforce. Outsourcers that invested in these countries are now faced with a difficult choice: reduce service levels, increase rates, or lose money. You can imagine how well that story played in the boardrooms of their clients.

The example illustrates why companies must manage their supply carefully. The consequences of disruptions in business services are no less serious than the failed delivery of material that forces a manufacturing plant to close down, or a network outage that creates havoc in a financial institution. Improved supply management is why many companies that outsource have shifted from a procurement or vendor management mindset to a partnership mind-set. Partnership can take on different forms, depending on the needs, the maturity level of the partners, and so on, but one thing that partnership always means is that the outsourcing company takes a vested interest in the success and profitability of the outsourcing provider. The company expects the outsourcer to care about its well-being and success. Why should this be a one-way street? Although true partnership in outsourcing is rarely achieved, those companies that do achieve it are far more satisfied with their outsourcing efforts than those that don't.

The supply management component of the Sourcing Management Model addresses the effective management of the resources that the outsourcing market offers its clients, specifically in the following areas:

PARTNER RELATIONSHIP MANAGEMENT

This is not unlike customer relationship management in that both require open and honest communication, take a win-win approach to problems and solutions, strive for fair treatment of individuals and their interests, and aim at a positive overall experience. However, partner relationship management is also counterintuitive. Although your company may be paying good money for the services provided, at the end of the day, you are still competing for the attention and the best resources and services your outsourcer can provide to all its other customers. A good rule of thumb to gauge effectiveness of partner relationship management is to ask: Would you put the same people you have in this role in a customer relationship role? If so, you are probably bringing the right skills and aptitudes to the function; if not, you are most likely still practicing vendor management rather than relationship management.

SETTING PARTNERSHIP OBJECTIVES

Companies succeeding at outsourcing set explicit, measurable targets for each relationship and monitor them consistently and in depth. The objectives in the most successful companies are also bidirectional, meaning that objectives are set for both parties, and defined in terms of business outcomes rather than operational metrics. Some examples of strong partnership objectives include:

- Realized value (e.g., a 10 percent increase in ROI from projects executed by the outsourcer on behalf of the client).
- Customer/user experience (e.g., a 10 percent improvement in help desk satisfaction numbers).
- Financial (e.g., a 3 percent decrease in unit cost; growth of commercial relationship to $50 million).

- Relative positioning (e.g., become one of the outsourcer's top 10 customers; enter into the client's preferred partner category).

- Service performance (e.g., zero material business disruptions).

MANAGING SUPPLY INFRACTIONS

Managing supply infractions requires some counterintuitive thinking and behavior. When a service level agreement (SLA) is breached, the first response is to immediately assign blame and, if appropriate, a penalty, but both of these actions ignore the fact that these companies are in a relationship, not just bound by a contract, and they should be looking to solve the problem, not just point fingers. Supply managers should look at the total number of infractions by a partner and base their decision for action on whether there seems to be a systemic problem or a series of isolated incidents. They should also consider whether the infraction had any business impact; if not, perhaps the SLA needs to be modified.

The situation can quickly begin to strain the relationship, or perhaps even destroy it altogether, if emotions around the incident dominate the response. The same result could ensue if the company insists on adhering strictly to the contractual terms and does not consider real-world impacts. It is the supply manager's job to understand the infraction, why it happened, and what can be done to resolve it, and then *help* the partner address it permanently. The supply manager is in a better position to do this than the people or function that suffered the incident, because the manager is a step removed (and likely less emotional about it) and because it is the manager's key responsibility to broker win-win solutions.

PARTNER ADVOCACY

Partner advocacy is one of the most difficult behaviors to learn. Supply managers have the difficult and often politically charged roles of promoting and marketing the partner's business outcomes inside the enterprise. They explain to consumers how their behaviors may be resulting in higher costs or compromised service levels. They are always on the lookout for opportunities to expand the contributions of the partner to company value. And they coach the partner on the corporate environment and performance expectations in order to promote the mutual success of the relationship. Supply managers must have thick skins. They are likely to be on the receiving end of attacks and accusations such as that reported by one manager who was labeled a traitor for his efforts to teach his colleagues to become wiser consumers of an outsourcer's services. One relationship manager joked that his own company viewed him as "inside sales" for the outsourcer. This is probably an indication that he was doing his job well. Good supply managers have a passion for doing what is right and not worrying about whether they are popular.

Because the mission of the supply manager may not make apparent sense to the company, and because there will inevitably be resistance and skepticism around partner advocacy, companies need to take specific steps to help it succeed. For example, supply managers must be compensated, in part, on the performance and value contribution of their assigned partners.

MARKET INTELLIGENCE

Market intelligence is a critical activity for supply management, and it involves constantly asking and answering the following questions:

- *What is the state of the art in the specific processes or functions we outsource, or are planning to outsource?* Are we confident the provider is delivering competitively with the industry? The cost and performance implications from the best-performing relationships to the worst-performing relationships can differ by orders of magnitude, and effective supply management means knowing whether a company's partners follow leading industry practices.

- *How do your partners make money?* Are they making money from their relationship with your company? Surprisingly, many companies in Project LAO spoke of having strong partnerships and healthy relationships, but had no firm data on whether they are a profitable client for their outsourcer. You need to understand the drivers of cost and margin in the outsourcer in order to be able to act to make them a more profitable concern. In a true partnership, each side knows and understands how its partner makes money, and each works actively to improve the other's business performance.

- *What is the industry doing?* Do you know whether a new proposal from your existing partner is a leading, following, or lagging industry practice? What best practices have others deployed that you could leverage? What best practices have you deployed that you absolutely do not want your competitors to have access to? Sound intelligence about industry practices and clear understanding of your position

relative to the latest innovations are the contributions of robust outsourcing market intelligence.

- *What are other industries doing?* Innovation can come from
  outside your industry. Combining your company's
  unique capabilities with the efficiencies and differentia-
  tors of your outsourcer can lead to significant value improvements. One of the best ways to seek and identify
  those value opportunities is to constantly monitor how
  other industries are leveraging their outsourcing partnerships. You can find out what to do next—as well as what
  to avoid doing.

- *What are the geopolitical and socioeconomic implications of
  sourcing choices on your business?* Globalization has made
  it possible—and in many cases desirable—to spread your
  workforce across multiple regions. Market intelligence
  has the responsibility of anticipating certain scenarios,
  communicating the impact they may have, and developing work-arounds and risk mitigation strategies. Can
  your market intelligence answer questions such as: What
  would the impact be of a general strike in Mumbai on
  our offshore outsourcing activities? What is the likelihood of war or other political conflicts impacting our
  business continuity? Can outsourcing in China be used
  as a bridge to better serve the enormous Chinese customer market? What would be the effect of protectionist
  legislation on our outsourcing endeavors?

Effective supply management paves the way for strong partnerships, which in turn results in increased customer and
shareholder value for both the client and the outsourcer. Many
companies that are already several years into their outsourcing

relationships have learned that practicing rigorous supply management makes the difference between the relationship maturing into a sustainable, profitable endeavor or breaking down into a bitter blame game.

Sourcing Program Management

"We found over $15 million in opportunity just by looking at all of our outsourcing deals together for the first time. We learned a few things: We had no idea we were already outsourcing to the tune of $200 million. Our expectations of outsourcers by department varied significantly, and worst of all, we were paying nearly twice as much to the same vendor for the same service in a different business unit! We are now on a path to managing outsourcing as a cohesive enterprise initiative, and each relationship as an asset."

—Newly named head of an enterprise outsourcing PMO

It is striking that outsourcing alone among recent business trends has escaped the rigor of disciplined program management. Although few if any companies would enter a reengineering effort, an e-business transformation, or an ERP implementation without a well-defined program structure, outsourcing is still viewed by most companies as a transaction to be completed, not a program. In reality, successful outsourcing is best viewed as a long-term journey, a complex initiative that changes the fundamental operating model of the company that uses it.

Program management tends to have multiple interpretations (and misinterpretations) depending on where it is used. We define program management as "the discipline of executing complex, multistream change initiatives that consume significant enterprise resources." The people, processes, and tools that make up the discipline of program management focus primarily on a single objective: realizing the business value of the initiative. Outsourcing program management involves research, due diligence, selection, activation, ongoing management, and termination of external sources of talent (human capital) to realize benefits in cost, focus, flexibility, or innovation for the corporation.

Drawing on experiences of more than three dozen companies with varying degrees of outsourcing program management, Concours developed a leading practice framework within the Sourcing Management Model, consisting of the following components:

PROGRAM PLANNING

Program planning involves the sequencing of activities, assignment of resources, and deployment of tools that will lead to the achievement of desired business outcomes. Often referred to as *road mapping*, program planning breaks the outsourcing marathon into a series of manageable sprints, each of which can be readily and exactly measured. Program planning also involves estimating and maintaining the budget, and gaining appropriate buy-in from the various stakeholders before a segment of work is begun. Program planning demands that the desired business outcomes be articulated. Most companies feel they have strong expertise in this area, but many fail to realize that to be successful in life after outsourcing they must clearly define the outsourcing end state so people will recognize when they get there.

OUTSOURCING

VIEWING PARTNER RELATIONSHIPS AS A PORTFOLIO

The portfolio is segmented into classes (much like asset classes in an investment portfolio) or channels, and actively managed for performance. If one partner in the portfolio underperforms relative to expectations, it can be divested and replaced with a more promising partner. Similarly, when a partner exceeds expectations, that success is thoroughly mined. Viewing active partners from a portfolio perspective means that your company views its outsourcing relationships as assets, to be stewarded and managed optimally on behalf of shareholders. Managing partners in a portfolio requires effective governance because it requires decisions about which partners to accept into the portfolio, which ones to expel from it, and which ones to move between the defined classes of relationships. Making each partner aware that you manage them as a portfolio tells them you are assessing them relative to their competitors and peers, and reminds them that there are both rewards and consequences related to their ability to help your company achieve its desired business outcomes.

EXECUTING MAJOR TRANSACTIONS

Major transactions include the award of a significant piece of business to a new or existing partner, or the elimination of a partner from the portfolio. Both are difficult. Major transactions tend to be months-long projects in and of themselves. Major transactions inevitably affect a number of the legacy outsourcing skills and processes. Requirement specification, negotiation, pricing, legal contracting, and transition support would typically be considered major transactions. This small component of the model gets disproportionate attention, energy, and resources. Although the importance of executing sound transactions should not be minimized, it is wise to remember that the day the deal is signed and both parties let out sighs of relief and throw big parties, *no value has been realized.* Practitioners agree almost universally that this is the point at which the hard work begins. Outsourcers and their clients alike do a disservice to their shareholders and the potential of their relationship if they take their eyes off the road ahead at this time. Similarly, nobody wants to think about what happens if the relationship turns out to be a disaster. Although you should be lucky enough never to have to use them, the processes, policies, and procedures for terminating a relationship have to be ready to go at a moment's notice.

RISK MANAGEMENT

Among the top concerns of nearly every company engaging in outsourcing, risk management is, arguably, more operational than programmatic, and although it might belong in the next component of the Sourcing Management Model, risk increases and decreases through the various phases of the life cycle. Generally, companies divide risk into a few categories, including financial, political, regulatory, service impact, and business impact. Segmentation of the types of risk helps identify and prioritize specific courses of action, as well as enable the measurement of exposure at any time. Ideally, many risks can be permanently retired, or fully mitigated, leaving bandwidth to manage the next set of risks. However, regardless of where risk management sits in the model, you will need to monitor and mitigate risks continuously, not just when the transaction is being planned and negotiated.

PROCESS IMPROVEMENT

If the Sourcing Management Model is largely an engine of processes that lead to success in life after outsourcing, then process improvement is the mechanism for keeping it finely tuned. Although there are lots of different names for this type of activity (six sigma, continuous improvement, reengineering, process excellence, etc.), all are valid frameworks for making processes efficient and effective. As organizations learn the various lessons of outsourcing, they must continuously tweak the process model that supports them. An example of a sourcing process model can be seen in Figure 6.4. Your processes for sourcing management may or may not be the same as the ones pictured here. It is actually more important that you assign ownership for each process you do have and ensure that owners are encouraged and rewarded for constantly challenging the status quo.

Sourcing management, in its current iteration, is still relatively new, and most companies will not get everything right the first time. Effective management of the outsourcing program (which is itself a process) makes the company a better outsourcer, but it also can drive it to the point of excellence, to the point where you can legitimately claim that your ability to acquire, manage, and dispose of third-party talent is a competitive differentiator. CEOs may not immediately buy into the notion that outsourcing should be a distinguishing capability of the corporation, but given that outsourcing typically deals with talent, cost, and service quality, would that same CEO argue for mediocre talent, average costs, and simply satisfactory service quality?

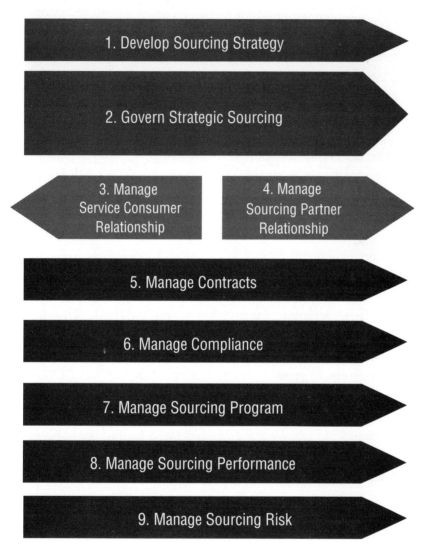

Figure 6.4   Sample Sourcing Process Model

PROGRAM COMMUNICATIONS

Many firms seem to underestimate the importance and sensitivity (not to mention the volume) of outsourcing-related communications. It may be that the often secretive nature of the deal-making phase of the life cycle carries over after the deal is done, but it is at this point—after the deal has been made—that communications must ramp up. Employees have hundreds of questions, some about the services (Will I experience the same service levels? Whom do I go to now when my mouse freezes up?), but perhaps many more about their futures (How will my job change as a result of outsourcing? Am I next?).

Employees are not the only people who have questions and need answers. Senior executives want to hear about how the outsourcing is going; the partner wants feedback. The media want comments and interviews; the partner wants to do press releases. The list goes on. A central communications function for all things outsourcing is crucial to avoiding potentially devastating missteps, such as issuing contradictory messages or allowing each department head to present his or her own spin on the situation to employees as a result of a lack of common talking points.

The communications challenges accompanying outsourcing are very similar to those that accompany other major change initiatives—except perhaps for the emotion that outsourcing triggers, because you are often dealing with people's livelihood in one way or another. It is important to recognize this and make sure the best communications skills and tools available are being centrally deployed in such a way that promotes the success of the outsourcing efforts.

Sourcing Operations Management

"Do you mean to tell me that we cannot certify our financial results because our outsourcer is not compliant?"

> *—An unhappy CEO to her CFO, upon discovering that there was no way to guarantee that their outsourced service provider had met all the criteria for Sarbanes-Oxley certification*

Sometimes it is the operational basics that cause trouble, such as in the earlier example. Although an oversight of this magnitude is rare (and unforgivable for both the provider and the buyer of the outsourced services), they do happen. Sourcing operations management deals with making sure incidents like this are very, very uncommon.

The day-to-day, steady-state activities of outsourcing—the sourcing operations—generally do not vary significantly in effort over the course of a year, and are independent of new transactions or initiatives. Sourcing operations management activities include:

MEASUREMENT AND REPORTING

Without measurement, the company has no idea whether the desired business outcomes are being achieved. Without reporting, whatever is known about the performance of the outsourcing partner remains useless. Scorecards are one very effective method for assessing outsourcing, and the most successful outsourcing companies develop and tweak their scorecards over time. Figure 6.5 is an example of an effective scorecard. Note that the measurements take a balanced view of the performance of the total sourc-

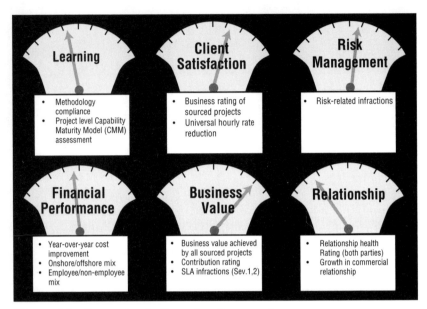

Figure 6.5   Example of a Sourcing Scorecard

ing program, not just the performance of one provider. Note also in the scorecard that operational metrics are not prominent. Instead, there is far greater emphasis on business impact, the real value (or lack thereof) of outsourcing when all is said and done.

A common measurement practice is for companies to assess the sourcing partner's performance, but scorecards must measure the performance of both parties in the partnership to deliver maximum utility. Although companies may feel a certain level of discomfort in exposing themselves to evaluations by their service providers, measurement is not personal, nor is it a permanent indictment. Done well, measurement is the only reliable way to expose gaps in performance on either side. If certain company actions are making it difficult for the partner to achieve its promised performance, you should know about it. If minor changes in demand behavior, for example, could translate into major savings in service delivery, you need to know about it. Of course, you should also rely on a more intuitive measure of a partner's performance, one that may not be easily measured.

Mature companies with more than one provider also view partner data in aggregate: How successful is our overall sourcing program? Why is partner A so successful in maintaining service levels and partner B so poor at it? What can we then learn from our experience with partner A to help partner B raise its game? Reporting on outsourcing performance is key to capturing the value. The point is to present a total view of the outsourcing efforts in a way that is digestible and actionable by the audience.

AUDIT AND COMPLIANCE

In a Sarbanes-Oxley world, companies are responsible for identifying and fixing compliance gaps. To do this right, you must perform joint compliance planning with your providers, and be sure that your internal and external audit processes are fully integrated with your outsourcers' processes and functions as well. The good news is that outsourcers in general are well aware of the need for audit and compliance, and they have significantly improved their capabilities in this arena. The bad news is that it is time-consuming; you must be cautious not to divert attention from more profitable activities and you must avoid increasing the cost of an outsourced solution. Companies that lack this capability as part of their overall outsourcing management model are exposing themselves to unacceptable risk and their executives to an early career end.

CONTRACT MANAGEMENT

When used interchangeably (and erroneously) with sourcing management, the mistakes can be costly. In the scorecard model, contract management is only one slice of the total sourcing management picture. The fact is that contract management is often the *only* component of the model in place, which reflects the failure to move beyond vendor management to relationship management. Worse yet, in many cases, companies have actually abdicated monitoring the outcomes of the outsourcing effort to the outsourcer, all the company cares about is that contract terms are met. However, if the contract was a bad one, then using the terms of that contract as measurement criteria is a waste of time. If actual needs have changed and the contract has fallen behind, then measuring to the contract is a waste of time. The message is clear: Blindly enforcing a contract is just as risky as not having a contract all.

Good contract management means making the contract a living document, one that changes with business needs and the discovery of better ways to do things. One of the challenges in contract management is to capture the improvements resulting from "handshake" deals (which are often completely reasonable), and ensuring that they become reflected in the language of the contract as amendments. It is a wiser course of action, by the way, to become aware of informal agreements and to integrate them into the legal framework of the relationship than to ignore them.

At the end of the day, contract managers must be the enforcers, protecting your company's best interests in the most difficult situations and standing ready to proceed with drastic measures when all other avenues fail to resolve the serious issues in the relationship. If all they do is enforcement, then they are performing only half of their job; the other half is to shepherd the complex, onerous, and exhaustive legal document so that it helps drive flexibility to meet business outcomes for both parties involved. The contract may specify the business outcomes, but often it also contains the language that ensures you never meet them. Contract managers need to recognize, raise, and resolve these conflicts.

PROCESS MANAGEMENT

So now that you have built a powerful engine for your sourcing efforts, how do you keep it performing at its peak? Process management focuses on the enforcement of the processes that have been defined and implemented. Governance, in addition to being a management discipline, is a process. It has a number of steps that follow in sequence, for example: identifying the need for a decision, assessing and documenting its impact, teeing it up for discussion in a governance council, making the decision itself, assigning ownership for its implementation, and making sure it does get implemented. How do you make sure that all these steps are completed? By implementing rigorous process management, which collects process metrics (all good processes have defined outcomes that can be measured) and ensures that processes are performing as they should. If you added a new partner to the partner portfolio, you would not want the appropriate approvals skipped, nor would you allow it to go through without appropriate review by legal counsel. Avoiding these pitfalls is the hallmark of well-managed outsourcing processes.

For all the effort that goes into making outsourcing deals, very little attention is devoted to the few simple things that keep those deals sound, compliant, and mutually beneficial.

When cohesively deployed, the components of outsourcing operations management protect your company's investment in outsourcing and help ensure the smooth running of your outsourcing engine. Just as importantly, they constantly monitor the environment for exceptions and infractions that need the attention of management, the outsourcer, or both.

Outsourcing Demand Management

A CIO explained that in his company's first year of outsourcing a significant part of the application development and maintenance (ADM) function, throughput actually decreased by almost 40 percent (the goal had been a 20 percent increase). When he investigated, he found the outsourcers were meeting and exceeding all the agreed-to service levels. Root cause analysis led to discovering that although each business unit that consumed ADM services had agreed to provide requirements specifications in a standard template, with very specific completion criteria, that agreement had been forgotten. Each business unit continued to use its old process for delivering specifications for development—one of these processes was completely undocumented and historically handled entirely by phone conversations. As a result, the outsourcers had the additional complexity of trying to find all of the information they needed before they could even understand the specification, which slowed down the entire development life cycle.

This company learned an important lesson about living up to its commitments in order to get desired results (it also learned that had throughput been one of the explicit performance objectives for the outsourcer, it could have avoided the issue altogether). It is the responsibility of demand management to make sure that service consumers live up to their end of the bargain.

Many participants in Project LAO were candid in their self-assessment, and one of the most common themes was the underestimation of the challenges of demand management. In most cases in which this was true, a lot of work went into establishing a strong relationship, developing a good, flexible contract, and preparing the transitioned or severed employees for the change. However, rarely do organizations spend enough time preparing the consumers of the services they outsource.

The principal goal of demand management is to help your company be the very best *consumer* of outsourced services that it can be. When we hear the most successful outsourcing providers remark, "Company X really knows how to work with us. Work requests are clear, the environment is collaborative, and their expectations of us are always well known—they get much more value from our service offerings. Why can't our other clients be like that?" we know that strong demand management is the reason for their achieving high levels of satisfaction. Good demand management also differentiates your company among the providers and other customers as a smart buyer. Outsourcers respond to this (in many cases subconsciously) by assigning their A teams to such clients. The outsourcer's employees compete for a slot at an account where the demand is known to be reasonably managed. Better talent usually brings better results, so just developing the capability to manage the service consumers can trigger a fortunate and rewarding chain of events.

Demand management does not just mean giving the outsourcer what it wants. More likely, it means making sure that consumers of the services provided are satisfied with their service levels and knowledgeable about the impact of their decisions on the benefits (or lack thereof) of their outsourcing arrangements. Managing demand well also means continuously interacting and improving upon the performance goals expected of the provider.

Finally, demand management is about partner advocacy. A few organizations have grown so enamored of their large outsourcing deals that they actually compromise their business's influence, power, and authority over their outsourcers. However, in the vast majority of deals there is a lack of partner advocacy that leads to unmet expectations and suboptimal results.

Demand management components are discussed next.

RETAINED PROCESS INTEGRATION

Always a challenge for organizations near the beginning of their outsourcing journey, retained process integration also poses problems for companies with significant experience, because they have not seamlessly integrated their outsourced and retained processes. Suppose you have outsourced finance and accounting transactions, but not purchasing. At some point, the goods or services you procure will have to be paid through accounts payable processes owned by your outsourcer. How do you make sure that information flows seamlessly from your in-house purchasing group to your outsourced (and possibly remote) finance group? What systems must interact in order to get the purchase order booked and the invoice paid? Who is accountable for end-to-end process performance?

Even when the intention is to outsource a complete process (e.g., order to cash or application development and maintenance), there will always be formal and informal interactions with other processes executed within the company. Not surprisingly, outsourcers are reluctant to agree to targets that reflect performance of processes they participate in but do not own.

However, companies must resist the temptation to oversegment processes as a result of outsourcing. In a partnership, you should hold each other mutually accountable for the overall process performance that leads to business impact.

Most companies understand the value of process design and process improvement, so there is no need to cover it here. Chances are your company already employs a robust methodology to integrate, reengineer, and continuously improve your processes. That same methodology should be used to ensure that process handoffs with outsourcers are seamless and smooth, the business impact of each process is measured regardless of who executes which pieces, and there is one overall process model for the company that includes both internal and outsourced activities. If you are successful, you should never have to hear things like, "Well, we would have delivered the project on time, but our outsourcer did not provide the inputs in the format we requested," or "We are meeting all our SLAs, but when we hand off to your employees, we don't know what happens—it is a black hole."

CONSUMER RELATIONSHIP MANAGEMENT

This is the interaction of the groups inside and outside the company that use the outsourced services. Setting expectations for the consumers of outsourced services is perhaps the most frequent point of failure within demand management. What it requires should be familiar:

- Understand what is a win for your service consumers and help your service providers (outsourcers) deliver it.
- Act upon issues, complaints, and feedback quickly and keep the initiator informed.

- Understand the service consumers' current and future business needs and take the initiative to develop outsourced services that meet them. Don't wait for them to ask for a so-called emergency project that really was planned a year ago.

- Represent the service consumers' best interests to the outsourcer and the sourcing management group. Be an advocate for their concerns and needs and work to resolve their issues quickly. Find compelling ways to articulate the value proposition of combining their capabilities with the outsourcers.

None of this is rocket science. It is simply the application of sound practices for customer management to service consumers. Why doesn't the outsourcer do this? To some extent, they should, but companies are concerned about not having a single point of contact on either end for good reason: Do you want your outsourcer talking to every last executive vice president who has a problem? Do you want the consumers making side deals with outsourcers that you are not aware of? (This is extremely common, by the way.) You should have a single place where all issues and triumphs are dealt with, and an implicit high-trust working relationship between the demand manager and the service consumer.

However, the most important role that demand management plays is in making sure that the consumers live up to their end of the bargain. Because they are also writing the checks, this is one of the most diplomatically challenging roles in the enterprise. Successful companies have found a way to place a value-added buffer between the outsourcer and its ultimate customers. Although this role and function may eventually disappear as both demand and supply maturity increase, for the foreseeable future the likelihood is that service consumers and service providers will not be ready to interact in an unmanaged setting.

DEMAND CONSULTING

As the name implies, demand consulting means helping your business become a better consumer of outsourced services. Demand consultants work with the service consumers to frame issues and problems in a way that allows service providers to add the most value. Unlike consumer relationship management, demand consulting is not a steady-state process; rather, it provides the temporary guidance and support that businesses need when deciding how, when, and from whom to source. This subcomponent of the model requires a consultative, analytical skill set and a rigorous problem-solving methodology, in addition to depth of understanding of the service consumer's business problems. Demand consulting can be activated to help resolve small problems—such as service requisition issues—or large ones—such as deciding which partner to award a significant new piece of outsourcing business.

The objective in most cases is to help businesses leverage the maximum possible value from their outsourcing relationships. Whenever ideas that allow a company to differentiate its capabilities by adding the outsourcer's service offerings, demand consulting plays an even more important role by helping the company reconfigure outsourcing services in ways that capture that value.

OUTSOURCING

CAPTURE AND FULFILL DEMAND

Capture involves developing sophisticated forecasting tools and procedures. For example, if one desired outcome from outsourcing is the flexibility to ramp resources up or down when business needs change, companies need to develop an annual resource forecast, updated at least quarterly, that can be shared with their partners. Such a forecast might include small items (e.g., an efficiency project that will lead to a decrease in demand, requiring a lower head count from the outsourcer) or even transformational items (e.g., planned merger and acquisitions activity that will lead to a large spike in demand for a certain type of resource, such as an in-house supply chain transaction function in the acquired company that will be absorbed by the outsourcer). Either way, the information in the forecast can position the outsourcing partner to meet those needs. Although not every resource requirement change is predictable, capacity planning is the best way to sustain expected service levels and cost savings through times of turbulence.

Fulfilling demand involves determining how many partners you need, which ones have the required capabilities, which of the partners you already have can perform the work, which work requires new partners, and how quickly you can get them up and running. Applying some of the time-tested practices of manufacturing businesses has its place in the Sourcing Management Model. Although it is unwise to view outsourcing as a pure commodity, outsourcing resembles manufacturing insofar as the processes outsourced tend to be invisible to the end consumer, the tasks required tend to be repetitive and somewhat easy to automate, and the delivery of materials (in this case, resources) at the right time and at the right place is critical to the efficiency and profitability of the business.

MANAGING MULTIPARTNER INTERFACES

Companies using multiple outsourcing partners are often un-prepared to manage them. Managing expectations between a single outsourcing service provider and the service consumer is complex, but the work is exponentially harder with two, three, four, or more partners. Classic examples include the outsourcing of IT infrastructure to one partner and application development and maintenance to another, or the outsourcing of finance and accounting to one partner and systems support to another. These are not necessarily bad outsourcing decisions, but they do require special attention. Left unmanaged, these arrangements can quickly turn to ugly finger-pointing over who is responsible for what and why something did not turn out the way it was planned. Outsourcers naturally might not trust one another and might behave as rivals, with the consequences being both time-consuming and debilitating for your company, especially if your company is forced to mediate these relationships.

The good news is that these potential conflicts, usually occurring when two partners support the same area or initiative, can be avoided through careful planning and documentation of roles and expectations. The bad news is that you can never anticipate all the potential conflicts in a multipartner environment, and that may require assuming an ombudsman role to resolve them. When conflicts are resolved amicably, the solutions should become policy to avoid the same situations occurring again.

Benefits of the Sourcing Management Model

All companies, regardless of the scale or locale of their outsourcing activity, can apply the Sourcing Management Model. There are inflection points: A billion-dollar deal might require a significant dedicated staff and lots of visibility to the management of the company whereas a $10 million deal might require a very small staff and the sponsorship of just one or two key executives to perform all those activities. Most companies engaged in outsourcing today have many, but not all, of the Sourcing Management Model components already in place.

The Sourcing Management Model, when properly implemented, can significantly improve the odds of a company being in the successful third that do accomplish their outsourcing-related business outcomes. More importantly, though, those companies that make the management of outsourcing a core competency will develop an advantage in the marketplace, providing better results, improved service levels, and ultimately shareholder returns.

Because the Sourcing Management Model is difficult to implement, companies that master it will have, for a limited time, competitive advantage over those that have not. They will not only be more sophisticated consumers of outsourcing than their industry peers, they will also be better positioned to manage a global talent pool, which is vital to competing in a world economy.

This model captures the best practices of companies that have been successful in their outsourcing endeavors, and shows how all the required pieces fit together. Of course, individual implementations will vary somewhat based on industry, specific goals, and existing or developed intellectual capital of a given company.

Key Points to Remember

- The Sourcing Management Model is difficult to implement and requires significant commitments of energy, time, leadership, and resources, but when the right model for your company is in place, the risks of outsourcing decrease and the value increases. The ultimate result is that you have a model that is very difficult to imitate because it is unique, and, therefore, a competitive advantage in sourcing labor and talent.

- Successful life after outsourcing requires adopting many counterintuitive behaviors, such as intentionally becoming one of your outsourcing partner's best customers by managing to the relationship and not the contract, or looking to resolve SLA problems rather than finger-pointing and immediately resorting to penalties, even if they are allowed in the agreement.

- Successful life after outsourcing requires applying many things you already know (e.g., manufacturing excellence) to outsourcing.

- The Sourcing Management Model can grow with you as you add more partners or decide to manage a global pool of talent that includes internal and outsourced staff.

- Sourcing is a relationship, not a piece of paper or a commodity to be purchased. Thinking about and treating the outsourcing provider as a partner can deliver results that exceed the contract expectations and add considerably to the intellectual capital available to you.

CHAPTER

7

More from the Experts

Transforming the Next Generation of Outsourcing

IBM and the Outsourcing Institute

Outsourcing began as a way for companies to cut costs and gain access to expertise that was unavailable internally. This was accomplished by delegating components of a business process to an outside vendor, which enabled management to spend more time focusing on core activities. This model is in wide use today and remains very effective for businesses to increase their overall productivity.

Today's information technology (IT) environments present a number of challenges to well-directed efforts to merge IT with business. Many companies are realizing that, if IT is truly going to support their strategic business objectives, they need a way to easily manage their technology. The concept of on-demand outsourcing allows corporate executives and IT personnel not only to consolidate and integrate their systems, but also to simplify IT management and reduce costs. Further, the idea of implementing an outsourced on-demand utility solution that permits pooling IT resources company-wide, and gaining an ability to track usage on a per-business-unit basis is highly appealing to companies looking to substantially reduce total cost of ownership.

Although many companies are intrigued by the possibilities of on-demand outsourcing, it is also important to remember that this new phase of outsourcing is still evolving. With the exception of several early adopters and selected providers, today's computing infrastructure is not prepared to support a highly dynamic, responsive, integrated business environment. Innovative companies are planning for this business transformation through the adoption of services-oriented architectures—a new way of thinking of business processes and IT infrastructure.

Comments Frank Casale, founder and CEO of the Outsourcing Institute, "It is critical that organizations that seek to leverage 'on demand' outsourcing services have a solid understanding of their business and technology requirements as they relate to their respective corporate visions."

For these reasons, many large enterprises seeking to reduce the cost and complexity of their IT environments are turning to IBM Global Services to help them design, build, and operate an on-demand IT environment. This type of transformational outsourcing is a strategy-based proposition and delves into the next generation of outsourcing.

Next-Generation Outsourcing— A Transformational Path to Business Value

As outsourcing matures, the tendency for organizations to enlist third-party management of all but the most mission-critical business operations continues to grow. There is also an increased desire to achieve the flexibility and agility to become on demand businesses. Progressive companies are looking to advanced outsourcing models, such as Business Transformation Outsourcing (BTO), as a key to help provide a catalyst for overall business transformation. As part of the next generation of outsourcing, providers that offer on-demand services will demonstrate that outsourcing goes beyond cost cutting and has become a strategic element in business transformation.

IDC recently reported that "although the traditional drivers of outsourcing—to reduce operational costs, improve IT flexibility, focus on core competencies and increase operational efficiency—still stand, [there is] mounting evidence that companies have turned to outsourcing for more strategic reasons."[1]

From e-procurement to e-learning to e-workplaces, transforming processes and integrating them into an end-to-end e-business model can create significant value. More and more organizations are utilizing the benefits of BTO to run the full course of transformational outsourcing. Companies are moving away from simply using outsourcing for improvements in operational excellence to strategically incorporating new business designs, and finally making the full transformation into a business that can move with the agility required to cater to customer demands and market fluctuations. "In fact, business transformation outsourcing can be viewed as one of a series of levers a company can pull to move it along on its journey to becoming an on-demand enterprise," comments Jim Gant, vice president of strategic outsourcing with IBM.

---

[1]IDC report, "Worldwide IS Outsourcing Market Forecast and Analysis, 2000–2005."

As a thought leader in innovation and front-runner in the movement toward next-generation outsourcing and the on-demand business, IBM Global Services has made huge strides in mainstreaming the way companies incorporate their IT infrastructure.

The On-Demand Enterprise

In this time of constant change and intense competition, corporate executives and IT personnel have no choice but to learn to survive and thrive in an environment of change. With pressure on corporate performance more intense than ever, business has reached a point where the need to act has run headfirst into the ability to act.

CAUSE AND EFFECT: THE CATALYST FOR ON-DEMAND

Since the earliest days of commerce, it has been possible to boil business down to a few fundamental elements: identifying or creating a market for an offering, creating the offering, supplying it to the customer, getting paid for it, and managing the customer relationship.

These fundamentals haven't changed—and those companies that remain focused on them will survive the toughest market conditions. Over the past decade, however, the changing business climate has had a profound effect on how companies do business and compete. For instance:

- Many industries, such as financial services, telecommunications, transportation, and utilities, have deregulated worldwide, opening the doors to new competition and consolidation.

- Initiatives such as the euro currency and North American Free Trade Agreement (NAFTA) have globalized business.
- The Internet and related network technologies have ushered in new business models.

It is the advent of these new, constantly changing business models that has brought us to the cusp of a major shift in business design and management thinking: the emergence of the on-demand enterprise.

The promise of on-demand is that companies or institutions can respond dynamically to virtually whatever business challenges arise. They can provide products and services in real time, adapt their cost structures and business processes to reduce risk, and drive business performance. They can optimize their IT infrastructures to cut costs and boost productivity. And they can be resilient, prepared for virtually whatever challenges may arise. The question often is not whether companies have on-demand attributes, but to what extent they have them and at what cost. On-demand business really is about responsiveness to customers—having the capacity to expand service offerings to get customers what they need, when they need it.

ON-DEMAND'S PIONEER

IBM has pioneered an emerging concept in the strategic outsourcing world by developing a model called e-business on demand™. This initiative was designed for businesses to be able to respond rapidly and productively to competitive pressures and other factors associated with an increasingly dynamic, globalized economy.

Engaging an IT outsourcing provider such as IBM not only allows businesses to realize significant cost reductions, it also helps:

- Accelerate speed to market and speed to delivery.
- Gain access to leading-edge skills, processes, and technology.
- Leverage economies of scale in a highly integrated environment.
- Benefit from best practices–based governance.
- Forge stronger links with partners, suppliers, and customers.
- Improve reliability and availability.
- Achieve a higher return on investment.

Additionally, IBM's strategic outsourcing services help companies realize flexibility and adaptability, and create a sound foundation for strategic e-business initiatives and business transformation. On-demand capabilities are tailored to cases in which IT demands vary by season, month, day, or even hour. Although traditional outsourcing engagements allow for capacity fluctuations on a stable curve, adding on-demand capabilities facilitates adjusting capacity to both predictable and unexpected demands in a dynamic fashion.

ACHIEVING TRANSFORMATION WHILE MAINTAINING OWNERSHIP

According to research completed by Cap Gemini Ernst & Young LLC (CGE&Y), management and IT consultants, and research analyst firm IDC, the increasing complexity and volatility of the business environment has compelled companies to evaluate their strategies, competencies, and resources and consider a transformational outsourcing approach: a long-term relationship that focuses on managing uncertainty. Fifty-two percent of companies surveyed said that transformational outsourcing helps make them more adaptable and flexible; 42 percent said that it helps bring about a business transformation; 40 percent said it helps add value by focusing on the core business; and 32 percent said it helps them achieve stronger financial performance.[2]

In the past, IT departments have found themselves struggling with inflexible legacy systems that quickly became outdated and continuing IT spending cuts. This environment made rapid change and market adaptability virtually impossible. By transforming the enterprise IT environment and its associated services, optimizing IT assets through automation, speedier deployment, and tighter links among IT services, business processes, and service levels, IBM is offering new capabilities that help enterprises achieve this transformation, providing clients with choices such as continuous support from IBM, while maintaining ownership and responsibility for their IT environments or options to transfer all or part ownership into an outsourcing arrangement. IBM is leading the IT sector in providing flexibility for clients.

Jim Gant comments on IBM's experience with early adopters of IT outsourcing, "We quickly recognized that each company

---

[2]Cap Gemini Ernst & Young press release, September 23, 2002, "New Study Finds Market Volatility Drives Companies to Evaluate Outsourcing as Strategic Management Tool to Transform Business."

approached becoming an on-demand business in a way and at a pace which best suited its needs and business strategy. For many companies, this meant that they wanted to move some applications to the on-demand model immediately, others later. However, companies wanted to accomplish this within the same relationship with IBM. In other words, the desired relationship remained an overall outsourcing agreement, with all the services identified and provided within the agreement. On-demand capabilities were thus part of the agreement, rather than something separate."

Gant continues, "Successful business transformation requires a road map for change, an infrastructure or application strategy (or both), and change management. IBM's on-demand and flexible-support philosophy provides each of these essential elements, paired with industry and IT expertise as well as insights gained from IBM's own transformation."

IBM UNIVERSAL MANAGEMENT INFRASTRUCTURE

Companies today are building their business strategies around Internet-based technologies, carefully choosing solutions that allow them to operate with agility and speed in what is rapidly becoming an on-demand world. At the same time, they are requiring that information technology (IT) contribute in measurable ways to the creation of value across the organization and deliver a solid return on investment (ROI).

A practical application of this strategy is IBM's e-business on demand™ initiative. Through e-business on demand™, IBM has created the Universal Management Infrastructure (UMI), an integration of IBM and other provider products (hardware and software), architecture, and best practices into a range of solutions for building and managing utility-based environments to meet customer-specific needs and preferences. Utility computing offers a compelling opportunity for companies to merge business with IT in support of their strategic goals. IBM is helping to lead the shift to utility computing, the delivery of business processes applications, and infrastructure based on service levels aligned with business priorities.

Based on open standards and delivered through a new category of IBM Global Services offerings, the UMI-enabled environment affords businesses the flexibility they need to take advantage of utility computing today, wherever companies are in their journeys toward becoming on-demand enterprises.

CAPABILITIES OF UMI

The UMI is an important step forward in IBM's e-business on-demand™ initiative to define multiple paths for companies to use based on their immediate and long-term needs. As a result, IBM has developed several road maps to choose from that include the delivery of business processes, applications, and infrastructure based on service levels aligned with business priorities. Delivered through an engagement led by IBM Global Services, the UMI-enabled environment provides the core functionality required to implement automation or IT management in complex e-business environments. It encompasses key automation capabilities integrated with open-standards–based IBM e-business infrastructure, making it a comprehensive framework for enabling utility computing.

The end goal for on-demand computing is to enable organizations to manage and integrate their business processes enterprise-wide, and in support of that goal IBM is building business-driven service management capabilities that will provide companies with all the tools needed to view IT resources in the context of their own business strategies. The UMI is one of these tools. Ultimately, with these capabilities, companies will be able to track usage; meter and bill utility units on a usage basis; audit license and usage compliance via policy- and service-based levels; and use self-service functions to check the status of service-level agreements (SLAs), utility performance, and billing and confirmation details. Specific capabilities of the UMI are:

- With the UMI's evolving business-driven service management capabilities, everything from performing maintenance to troubleshooting problems to gathering timely data can be simplified.
- The UMI features policy-based orchestration, which enhances an infrastructure's ability to automatically respond to business needs.
- Through the UMI's Web-based interface, companies can monitor their environment in real time and help ensure it is running within accepted parameters.
- The UMI security features include monitored and controlled access, as well as defined system-authorized levels, and security-enhanced software operating environments.

The UMI provisioning capability pools infrastructure resources, and then apportions and configures them on demand.

PROVIDING SIMPLIFICATION AND STANDARDIZATION

As IBM looks toward the future, it envisions a new generation of e-business called e-business on demand™. IBM believes it will fundamentally transform the way enterprises operate, allowing companies to adapt business processes so they can collaborate and communicate with suppliers, customers, and business partners in new ways.

Yet e-business on demand™ requires a new type of infrastructure, one unlike today's typical IT environment. An on-demand infrastructure will be based on open standards and Web services, integrate business processes end-to-end across an organization, leverage virtualized IT resources, and be self-managing. This infrastructure won't evolve overnight, but IBM has taken a huge step forward in laying a technical foundation for it with the UMI.

STRATEGIC OUTSOURCING ON DEMAND— KEY TO FLEXIBILITY

Incorporating on-demand into strategic outsourcing offers new capabilities that can be leveraged to further reduce IT costs through dynamic pricing models. The key to accessing these benefits is to understand that strategic outsourcing is not a one-size-fits-all proposition. Successful outsourcing relationships are flexible, innovative, and customizable. As a thought leader in this new territory, IBM developed on-demand models to address these issues. They are the Flexible Demand Option and the Flexible Support Option.

IBM FLEXIBLE DEMAND OPTION

The Flexible Demand Option offered by IBM provides companies with a standardized and automated IT infrastructure in a security-rich, partitioned IBM facility. Unique features of the solution include the fact that multiple clients can share the environment in order to capture significant cost savings. At the same time, security-rich partitioning and other techniques are designed to maintain privacy and integrity.

IBM Flexible Support Option—A Framework for Transformation   IBM understands that certain companies will want to retain more control over their IT environment and offers the Flexible Support Option as a viable solution. It helps enable companies to pool and optimize resources across business units while harnessing the efficiencies of rapid and responsive scaling. The IBM Flexible Support Option is available today in two ways:

1. A client can retain ownership for its IT environment (including facilities, equipment, staffing, and the like). IBM provides UMI services to the client so that the client can better manage the client environment.
2. A client can turn over the environment to IBM, and IBM will create a UMI-enabled environment dedicated to just that client.

The IBM Flexible Support Option helps an enterprise determine which key infrastructure components best support an on-demand computing environment, as well as the IT modifications necessary to generate the greatest business impact. Once decided, these changes are then prioritized and implemented within the UMI framework, enabling the enterprise to benefit from an IT infrastructure that is designed to be flexible, scalable, automated, and able to respond to ever-demanding business requirements.

Jim Gant adds, "The IBM Flexible Support Option is designed

to address the needs of enterprise clients who wish to take advantage of an advanced infrastructure management system while maintaining overall ownership of their IT environment, including equipment, software, and staff. Using the Flexible Support Option, CIOs can define how their IT infrastructure is allocated, utilized, and integrated within the business. Clients can also turn over their entire IT environment to IBM, as many of the early adopters have done. This alternative option provides an on-demand environment dedicated to a single client."

Making a Business Case for On Demand

Industry research indicates that greater flexibility can have positive consequences for corporations facing an uncertain future. The key to success in a turbulent situation is to be able to adapt to new situations rapidly—to react to sudden moves by competitors as they arise, but also to be able to take the initiative to use IT in new and innovative ways. IT executives facing continuous cuts to their IT spending might not have the luxury of being able to design flexibility into their IT portfolios. Eliminating or reducing IT support for business processes may also have a negative impact on functional performance.

The most obvious and commonplace solution to this problem has been to simply cut IT spending. Although an obvious solution, it is not by any means the best solution. Alternatively, IT outsourcing provides a solution, which helps to bolster flexibility while providing better control of IT costs. By choosing to selectively outsource, companies will see a continuous process improvement allowing the IT department to focus their remaining internal resources on strategic initiatives.

Focusing on the strategic portions of the IT business and outsourcing the process initiatives translate into greater IT business value in processes where flexibility is seen as a competitive necessity. In the short term, companies can see an improvement in their cost of service. More importantly, in the long run, companies can see the ability of their IT department to react favorably to external events as they arise.

The beauty and uniqueness of IBM's on-demand structure is that there are no real cookie-cutter models as there have been in the past with other types of outsourcing. Comments Frank Casale of the Outsourcing Institute, "You are either outsourcing or you are transforming—or you are doing both. When companies are about to embark upon a transformation strategy with an outside vendor, selecting a vendor that demonstrates extreme flexibility to accommodate its client's requirements should be the focus."

Transformational Outsourcing: Critical Success Factors

IBM's on-demand outsourcing model incorporates strategic goals into a transformational plan that allows as much or as little flexibility a company needs. This is a delicate balance and a complex structure that is still fairly unique in the outsourcing world. These services offered by IBM are a portion of the latest and upcoming phase of outsourcing: BTO.

Transformational outsourcing has several critical success factors that need to be present in order to achieve the optimum benefit for the client:

1. Be structured to deliver defined business outcomes that go beyond cost savings.

2. Deliver fundamental and sustained enhancements to the enterprise.

3. Span the breadth of the enterprise's operations.

4. Have flexible structures that utilize the best of the service provider's capabilities, which address the various needs clients will have.

Acknowledging that its on-demand structure was a transformational approach for companies, IBM chose to evolve its outsourcing delivery model and offer clients different types of infrastructure choices. The journey to the current on-demand structure was twofold:

1. IBM first determined how their on-demand initiative applied to strategic outsourcing.

2. IBM recognized that there would be several likely scenarios of adoption. As a result, it developed delivery models to address each of those scenarios.

History shows that IBM has been in the lead with the IT strategic/transformational outsourcing model, and has the advantage of access to results from its business thought leadership organization (Business Consulting Services).

Final Thoughts

Succeeding in today's business environment takes speed, efficiency, and flexibility. Companies must not only make an almost continual transformation to adapt to market forces, but as the change cycle continues to compress, enterprises are forced to be more flexible in their business models.

Within the past several years, many organizations have embraced business process and IT outsourcing as a way to control costs and focus on their core capabilities. However, traditional outsourcing may not be the best vehicle to deliver major business process transformation.

As a result, many executives are looking to take traditional outsourcing a step further, and they're asking for help—not only for running their business processes, but for transforming them to unlock hidden business value. Clients want more than just consulting or outsourcing; they need a partner that can work with them to deliver transformational change, and they are demanding greater accountability from their partners. This is a value that goes beyond simple cost savings.

To optimize the overall business impact of sourcing engagements, buyers must look for vendor qualities that exceed the current industry norm. States Casale, "Vendors that have attributes such as similar corporate culture, industry leadership and innovation, commitment to customer objectives, and bringing the value-addeds to the engagement form the benefits that now define the most successful outsourcing relationships."

Today, forward-looking companies in all types of situations face a number of common imperatives that result in the need for a different kind of partner—one with a vision to shape and accelerate change, share the risk of running and transforming their processes, and support them as a partner for the long term. IBM offers industry-leading capabilities to clients determined to succeed in a rapidly changing world.

About IBM Global Services

IBM Global Services is one of the world's largest information technology services and consulting provider, generating over $42 billion in 2003. Approximately 180,000 professionals serve clients in over 160 countries, providing a broad spectrum of clients' e-business needs—from the business transformation and industry expertise of IBM Business Consulting Services to hosting, infrastructure, technology design, and training services. IBM Global Services delivers integrated, flexible, and resilient processes—across companies and through business partners—that are designed to enable clients to optimize the opportunities of an on-demand business environment.

Outsourcing for Expertise

Scott Gerschwer

Manager, Media Relations, Pitney Bowes

---

*O*utsourcing has become a four-letter word in our society, triggering strong feelings about the future of work in America. Politicians have commandeered the term to suggest that it is a dark, un-American deed. During the last election, John Kerry claimed numerous times that the Bush administration outsourced the capture of Osama bin Laden rather than doing the job themselves. (If he had said "offshored" instead, who knows, he might have won the election.) But this country has a long history of outsourcing; if George Washington hadn't outsourced the training of his troops to European generals like Lafayette we might not even have a country.

Outsourcing is neither new nor nefarious. In most cases it's merely smart business. Executives know that if they are to succeed in an environment of increased competition and lower margins, they must increase productivity, take advantage of economies of scale, cut costs, and be more focused on their own core competencies. Among the many unintended consequences of Sarbanes-Oxley is a drive to centralize business services, reengineer systems and processes, and standardize on a global scale.

For shareholders, outsourcing is good because it occurs in a highly competitive environment, which holds down costs. It's also a good way to attain flexibility and do business more effectively. Successful outsourcing requires an organizational mindset that trades tactical control and maintains strategic control. Most importantly, the organization learns to share decision making with trusted partners. The most important benefit of outsourcing comes from leveraging the expertise of your partners. This is as true in the outsourcing of mail and document management as it is in the outsourcing of HR, IT, and accounting processes. Finding the right outsourcing partner to manage the flow of mail both within the organization and externally to customers and partners is key to your success, because these processes are so important to your business.

Outsourcing the Mail Process

There is a perceptual headwind that must be countered with some outreach to the public that mail is somehow losing its importance to businesses. Actually nothing could be further from the truth. The mail is an absolutely vital communication channel and will continue to be well into the future. The substitution of electronic channels for mail will continue to grow and mail will still be vital; just as radio found a lucrative role for itself after the rise of television, so will the mail. High-income groups, which are more likely to be wired than low-income groups, also get more mail. One recent marketing survey found that 76 percent of adults read their direct mail.

Another recent study, conducted by the United States Postal Service (USPS), shows that consumers are twice as likely to make an online purchase after receiving a printed catalog and spend 16 percent more than those who did not receive a catalog. Catalog recipients account for nearly 40 percent of all retail web sales despite making up just 22 percent of the total number of visitors. The combination of direct mail and the Web is highly effective, a fact not lost on marketers, who have made sure that Internet users get more mail than non-Internet users. The USPS expects that standard mail volume will increase by 4 percent in 2005.

Marrying First Class Mail and Technology

The USPS also expects that first-class mail volume will decrease by 2 percent in 2005, the continuance of a trend that began long ago. Conventional wisdom suggests that the downtrend in first class mail is due to people substituting e-mail for mail. Household-originated letter mail began to decline 50 to 60 years ago when telephone conversations replaced letter writing. It now constitutes about 10 percent of the mail stream in the United States. But the number of households increased by 24 percent over the past 15 years, which offsets the loss. And new technology has spurred the creation of new services that generate bills to be paid. The dynamic nature of the telephone industry is a good example: Consumers receive Internet, long distance, local, and wireless services from numerous vendors. Many people now may pay four bills instead of just one.

Greeting cards are a last holdout on the household-originated mail front. A survey conducted for Valentine's Day 2005 revealed 82 percent of card senders preferred to send their

Valentine's Day greetings by mail, compared to the 18 percent of those romantic devils who used e-mail. When the same group of respondents was asked how they would prefer to receive greetings, 86 percent said they prefer mail versus 14 percent who said an e-mail would suffice. For Mother's Day, your mom is not likely to accept an e-mail, so keep those cards and letters coming.

The volume of consumer-to-business mail will likely continue to drop, as the status quo in bill presentment and payment continues to be receiving the bill in hard copy and paying electronically. A recent study by Forrester Research shows that more than half of all the U.S. broadband households check their account balances on the Web, and one in three pays bills online. The Internet no doubt offers advantages in terms of speed, convenience, time, and other measures of efficiency, yet 26 percent of those who use the Internet to pay bills do so both online and offline. Of those, 34 percent do it more often online; 54 percent do it more often offline. However, even the most wired consumers still prefer to receive bills and statements in the mail. An example from a large mortgage insurer may be instructive about why.

Not long ago, in an effort to spur electronic bill payment and presentment, a financial services company raffled off a brand-new sports car, giving 10 raffle tickets to anyone signing up to receive and pay their bill online. The response was enormous: everyone wanted that car. So the company offered 20 more raffle tickets to anyone who agreed to turn off the paper statement. The response this time was dismal. The sentiment appeared to be: I'd love the car but I need my house. Having that paper bill around to serve as a reminder to pay was a security blanket that people were unwilling to give up.

Households that have Internet access both send and receive more transaction mail, even though the presence of a broadband Internet connection in the home should make them more susceptible to electronic transactions. In large measure, this apparent contradiction can be explained by the correlation of Internet access with income, education, and age.

In fact, age and responsibility are the most important indicators of mail usage. Younger adults (aged 18 to 24) receive, on average, approximately half as many pieces of mail received by 35 to 44 year-olds. As people age, their mail usage increases; as life grows more complex, bills and statements accompany that complexity. The peak mail usage years seem to be ages 45 to 54, where we receive about 15 percent more mail than our lifetime average. As these household heads continue to age, mail usage gradually declines. Generation after generation fits into this pattern as maturity brings new and increased responsibilities and individuals allocate their time to use the technology and channels appropriate to perform certain tasks.

Channel substitution will also be offset by volume, because business-originated communication is increasingly focused on the younger generation and the volume of advertising mail sent to this generation will be greater than the volume sent to older generations.

In conclusion, your business will need to utilize the mail stream for at least another 35 to 40 years. The question you need to answer now is whether you believe you have the expertise to manage this important channel yourself or if you need to find a partner. Remember, in his classic business book, *The Art of War*, Sun Tzu wrote that without alliances you are weak and vulnerable.

The Value of Mail

How's the quality of your product? What return do you generate from your mail-related activities? How efficient are your processes?

These questions should lead you to an inevitable decision: If you aren't getting all you can from the mailing process, you need help. If mail is not your core competency then you need to outsource it to an expert. Shareholders will forgive an insurance CEO for not understanding the intricacies of work sharing, but they won't forgive an insurance CEO for not being smart about dollars and cents. It's just as important to get value from the mail as from anything else. The quality of the product, whether you are getting each mail piece to work hard enough for you, is the question.

The variables that determine the success of a mail piece are numerous. Use of color, level of personalization, degree of data quality—in name and address but also in terms of personal preference—are all major factors for success. Is your mail stream well integrated with your CRM databases, your ERP systems, your key business processes? Are you using the mail to drive consumers to the Web for customer self-service to avoid costly service calls? Are you taking advantage of the white space on the envelope and on the bill itself? Is your mail system a closed loop system or are there loose ends?

Data Quality: The Need for Continuous Improvement

Let's take data quality as an example. IT professionals have used the maxim garbage in, garbage out (GIGO) for decades.

Yet the customer data that goes into CRM systems and is driving the communication apparatus is often outdated, corrupt, incomplete, and chock-full of errors or, at the very least, inconsistencies, and is stealing value from your business. A data quality effort isn't a one-shot deal. The USPS has given deep discounts for clean name and address data, yet found that even among those organizations that took the discounts the data was not getting sufficiently scrubbed. It is estimated that over 33 percent of addresses in customer databases have errors. "Undeliverable as addressed" mail cost the USPS $2.5 billion in 2004. Because of this, the USPS will likely require that mailers go beyond the traditional address cleansing solutions in order to attain address accuracy discounts.

Part of the problem is that organizations allow business units to create data warehouses, select data access software, and implement data management tools independently of one another, which leads to wasteful duplication as each subsystem captures an element of data in a slightly different way. Wasteful duplication and its remedies cost businesses an estimated $10 billion per year.

Inaccurate address data hurts your bottom line and is a detriment to customer satisfaction. According to Gartner, over the next two years data quality issues will limit the success of more than half of data warehouse projects. When outsourcing your mail process, make sure that your vendor has experience with extract, transform, and load (ETL) tools that can be used to integrate data from multiple source databases and transform it to a consistent format for storage in a target database.

One large financial institution that mails over 300 million first-class pieces and over a billion standard mail pieces per year successfully slashed its "undeliverable as addressed" mail by partnering with an application services provider, making nine million changes to data elements over a two-year period. And they aren't done yet! It's an ongoing process requiring continuous improvement, but it's worth the effort. High-quality data allows for better regulatory compliance, improved response rates, reduced costs, and, perhaps most important of all, true one-to-one marketing.

Personalization, Color, and Results

The shotgun approach to marketing is a thing of the past. The degree to which your mail can be personalized will largely determine its level of success. About a year ago a colleague and I visited the Automated Document Factory of a large financial services firm. In the middle of their floor was a tower that looked something like a windmill, but instead of four blades, it had 10 automated arms running up and down and across the structure. It had hundreds of cubbyholes filled with preprinted forms that the arms would grab and put together, creating a mail piece. I don't recall what its footprint was in terms of square feet or cost, but the thing was enormous, and now, two years later, it is quite obsolete.

Print-on-demand technology has created powerful capabilities for a new way to market. Digital color print is growing rapidly, specific job runs are growing smaller, and turnaround is faster, eliminating the need for the impersonal preprinted forms and massive run rates of the recent past.

Whereas a basic, black-and-white mail piece would generate an industry-acceptable response of less than 0.5 percent, the simple act of adding a name, the most basic level of personalization, increased the response rate by 44 percent. Adding color did about the same (45 percent). When name and color were combined, the response rate increased by 135 percent. Personalization and color produce a significant impact in the overall response.

But wait, there's more! Going beyond personalization by applying customer-specific information from your database increases the response rate by 500 percent. Referring to the recipient's recent purchases, for example, can provide significant uplift. So when looking for a vendor to help with your mailing and document processes, try to find one with knowledge of variable data. Not only is there room on the inside, but also the envelope itself is valuable real estate on which to billboard a targeted message.

Your variable data print runs will likely be smaller than the offset-driven print runs of the past, and your vendor should be flexible in its approach to handling output. Runs of 5,000 are increasingly becoming the norm, but capacity tends to spike; the vendor should have the capability to offload the overload to another facility when needed. A range of output devices is necessary. Finally, in case the worst occurs and your service is interrupted, a solid business continuity or business recovery plan is warranted. You don't want to pay for more capacity than you need, but when five hurricanes strike in one month, it's nice to have someone to turn to who can help you out of a jam. Your vendor should not be planning in a vacuum. See the business recovery plan before you sign.

Efficient Processes

An integrated mail and document strategy reduces costs, but deployment requires a comprehensive effort that incorporates desktop copying, printer, and fax; the handling of printed materials; reprographics; e-forms; and mail and postage. It's a complex process that ultimately delivers greater value than the sum of its parts might indicate. To complicate matters, there is often no common infrastructure or standard architecture for most of the business processes involved, with many applications run off of isolated legacy systems.

Management tracking systems need to be holistic solutions that consider all of the needs and challenges of document production facilities, from the beginning to the end of the process. They need to speak system-to-system, across the equipment and software solutions of multiple vendors, or they are useless. They need to institutionalize six sigma quality methodology across all operations and discard Band-Aid solutions that offer limited information and limited potential for cost savings and productivity improvements.

Six sigma specialists can deliver millions of dollars in productivity savings by reducing errors and running at zero defect levels of performance. Real-time, Web-enabled mail management systems allow executives to formulate and edit strategies and predict spikes in volume before they occur. If the vendor company can faithfully deliver options, a decision can be intelligently and jointly reached in order to prevent costly breakdowns. A best-site solution is another consideration. This allows your vendor to do some of the work on your premises while other work may be better done at a multiclient center, which provides a secure and specialized environment for each customer, but leverages the economies of scale that help keep production costs low.

Commingling mail is another option that makes use of work-sharing discounts offered by the postal service. In this scenario, your mail is added to batches of mail from other local businesses, which allows all participating businesses to take advantage of discounts. Because postage is approximately 70 percent of the cost of doing business by mail, this is a service that must be considered. Your vendor should have a plan to take your mail to presort houses for more efficient delivery.

Finally, the integration of mail with the rest of your business is a practical necessity. Seventy-five percent of customer-service calls relate to the billing statement. If you can drive even a third of these calls to your web site for self-service, you've gained a huge savings. Your mail stream is the circulatory system of your business. It must be connected to the brain to optimize decision making. It must be connected to the heart of your company to keep the revenue flowing. Adding intelligence into your mailing process, which can be accessed by simple barcodes printed right on the document, is a way to connect your mail stream to your key business processes.

Making It Work

The most successful outsourcing relationships are those in which the client company views the vendor as part of the team. The client wants the vendor to provide high-quality services in a timely manner, and a good vendor wants to meet those needs. Working together and respecting each other's role provides the best environment for successful outsourcing.

In conclusion, using outsourcing document management or mail services has many benefits. Vendors supply resources and technical expertise when needed, provide trained and experienced staff, offer proven processing procedures, ensure quality control and accuracy, adjust to the peaks and valleys for staff and equipment within changing volumes and schedules, and have cost- and time-saving suggestions. Selecting a good vendor is just the first step in successful outsourcing.

OUTSOURCING

For a positive experience, the following must also occur:

- A predetermined set of requirements is established by the customer and conveyed in writing with as much detail as possible to the vendor.

- Established communication protocols and liaisons designated to address any issues that may come up during processing. It's important to engineer the information flow between the client team and the vendor, with particular sensitivity to volume and scheduling, while providing a 360-degree feedback loop on a timely and regular basis that will ensure the quality of service. Protocols for addressing any problems should be established at the start of the project.

One other very important ingredient is for the client to provide a manager to qualify requirements, coordinate with the vendor, and manage in-house expectations. Having a knowledgeable support manager working on a project adds immeasurable value to the relationship. It also greatly increases the probability of a mutually successful outsourcing experience.

Never outsource your business to anyone that is so focused on the task at hand that they live in a vacuum. Outsource for expertise as well as service. Partner with someone who sweats the small stuff and who stays up nights thinking about how to squeeze more efficiency from the process, so you don't have to.

Human Resources Outsourcing Comes of Age

Scott Golas

Chief Strategy Officer and Senior Vice President,
Aon Human Resources Outsourcing

Human resources, like so many other core corporate functions, has come under intense scrutiny over the past two or three years as organizations look for ways to decrease costs and improve operational efficiencies. Costs associated with administering HR internally have soared as businesses rely on more sophisticated computer systems and software applications to perform standard HR functions. In addition to buying and maintaining these IT assets, organizations must attract and retain highly paid professionals who are skilled in the use of these systems. Added to these costs is the expense of complying with regulations such as the Sarbanes-Oxley Act and the Health Insurance Portability and Accountability Act (HIPAA).

In the effort to reduce spending on HR administration, a growing number of corporations and government agencies have turned to HR outsourcing (HRO). These organizations understand that by transferring the administration of personnel functions, such as payroll, insurance and other benefits, employee training and testing, compliance, relocation, and recruiting, to an outside firm, they can save millions of dollars a year. In fact, depending on current levels of HR-related spending, these organizations expect to save between 15 and 30 percent of their annual HR costs, through a variety of sources, such as:

- Increased operational efficiencies and access to resources, expanding return on investment (ROI) by leveraging economies of scale.
- Reduced capital spending, resulting from no longer having to upgrade aging back-office computer systems.
- Reduced payroll stemming from the elimination of internal jobs that oversee burdensome administrative tasks.

Although the potential cost reductions are impressive, the greatest benefits of HRO go well beyond savings and added efficiencies. Many organizations are finding that HRO delivers strategic value by transforming HR departments from cost centers to corporate resources equipped to facilitate growth and increase shareholder value. Outsourcing frees HR executives and departments from the time-consuming tasks of administering HR functions. It enables them to focus on allocating workforce resources more efficiently to achieve business objectives, and developing HR programs that are better aligned with the strategic goals of the business.

Therefore, while outsourcing can save a company a significant portion of its HR costs, the real long-term advantage is improving workforce performance by, for example, developing employees' skills so the organization can sell more products or service clients more efficiently, or implementing effective, well-aligned benefit programs.

Because the HR function maintains and manages nearly all of the organization's employee data, including job functions, expertise, backgrounds, skills, preferences, and compensation, it is in a better position than any other corporate function to understand the factors that determine and influence employee productivity. An HR function that is freed from low-priority tasks can truly help maximize workforce performance.

In an overall restricted corporate spending environment, CFOs and other senior finance executives expect managers to demonstrate measurable ROI for all major corporate initiatives, including outsourcing. Although cost reduction is a large part of the ROI equation, it shouldn't be the only measure.

When an organization is examining the returns from HRO, it is critical that the benefits are broader than cost savings. These organizations should identify strategic objectives, and then determine if those objectives are achieved through outsourcing.

Whereas many early HRO agreements were based solely on the projected cost savings for the client, today's outsourcing contracts should be based on the strategic value of the outsourcing relationship. In some cases, outsourcing may not fit with strategic goals. This is why it is imperative that, before embarking on an HR outsourcing arrangement, organizations achieve a solid understanding of costs and human resources service level requirements. The first step should involve a sourcing diagnostic, which is an evaluation of the current state of HR in the organization. The sourcing diagnostic will result in a snapshot capturing how and where the HR department is allocating it resources, in terms of people, processes, and technology. The second step should be an examination of the HR department's business objectives, along with a determination of the best ways to deliver on those objectives, either by outsourcing all or some HR components or by not outsourcing anything. It is important to remember that, although outsourcing is one service delivery model, it is not the only one.

The strategic value of HRO continues to grow as more organizations hire outside experts to take over these functions. Clearly, this strategy has moved beyond the point of simply being a good way to cut costs. For an increasing number of organizations, it has become the key to realizing the true potential of the workforce.

HRO Strategy: Stay Shallow or Go Deep?

Businesses face an important choice in the way they structure and pursue HRO strategies. It is a choice between a shallow or a deep HRO structure, and the implications for cost savings and operational advantages are significant.

The cost efficiency and strategic value resulting from a deep and comprehensive HRO plan may far outweigh any benefits stemming from a traditional, shallow approach. To make the choice, organizations must consider the critical differences between these two strategies.

DEEP HRO: A CASE STUDY

Company A has an annual revenue of $2 billion, and spends only 1 percent to 2 percent of that amount—or at least $20 million—on HR every year. In a shallow HRO approach, Company A targets a

15 percent to 30 percent savings of that $20 million. The result is a savings of approximately $5 million.

By leveraging deep HRO, Company A could achieve significantly more savings. It could also drive business value and leverage its workforce to combine strategy, consulting, design, and administration. Of the $2 billion in revenue, 40 percent to 60 percent is channeled into total workforce costs, which is roughly $800 million of the company's revenue. The goal of deep HRO is to save 5 percent to 20 percent of that $800 million. With a conservative estimated cost savings of 5 percent, Company A can gain $40 million, as opposed to $5 million, in cost efficiency, strategic value, and organizational improvement.

Shallow HRO, which has been popular for many years despite its financial and strategic drawbacks, involves the outsourcing of purely administrative duties, allowing the organization to focus on meeting its business objectives. The market for these services is $55 billion, and growing at a rate of 14 percent to 15 percent every year. This approach, favored among many business, is predicted to surpass the information technology (IT) outsourcing market in total market size in the near future.

Deep HRO is designed to increase productivity from workforce investments, dramatically increasing strategic and sustainable competitive advantage. Whereas shallow HRO contracts are limited to costs associated with direct HR-controlled administrative spending, the scope of deep HRO may allow employers to more closely manage HR-related employee costs outside the boundaries of the HR department. Employee training services, for example, represent costs that may be better managed, and consequently deliver greater value, if provided by an HRO professional specializing in integrated, comprehensive services.

Organizations are challenged to find deep HRO service providers with the depth and breadth of experience, as well as the talent and knowledge, to meet strategic HRO requirements. Those organizations seeking to create an effective, integrated, deep approach to outsourcing would benefit from a service provider specializing in deep HRO strategies and services. Combining traditional HRO methodologies with deep HRO vision and expertise will leverage the HR department and optimize the workforce.

The Deep HRO Methodology

If the key to gaining competitive advantage is optimizing the effectiveness of your workforce, instead of focusing merely on reducing administrative HR-related costs, the methodology used must encompass the key stages of the workforce life cycle:

- Source and select.
- Lead and manage.
- Reward and incentivize.
- Redeploy and retire.

SOURCE AND SELECT

The first step is finding and hiring the right people. Recruiting is a highly specialized business process, and it is important to use an integrated employment process outsourcing strategy designed to hire high-performance employees. This strategy begins with a standard and repeatable process that relieves the organization of multiple transactions and administrative burdens:

- *Candidate sourcing.* Active and passive candidate sourcing techniques will amass a qualified group of talented professionals, suited to strategic organizational needs.
- *Test and assessment administration.* Many companies use intensive selection and assessment tools to screen candidates, including behavioral, cognitive, and other employment-related testing. It is critical to use trained test administrators, certified interviewers, and assessors to evaluate and report on candidate qualifications.
- *Internal mobility.* Administering comprehensive internal staffing and employee referral programs will ensure that the organization is continually mined for experienced and high-performing employees.

LEAD AND MANAGE

Talented, ambitious employees want to learn, improve, and advance their careers. Fragmented training activities do not help employees gain the knowledge, expertise, and business acumen they need in order to excel in their careers. However, an HR team unhindered by daily administrative work can proactively respond to the learning and development needs of employees.

An outsource vendor should supply best practices and learning metrics to help the organization align performance and learning methodologies to business objectives:

- *Competency assessment and management.* It's vital to manage overall talent requirements across the organization by developing job profiles and corresponding talent profiles to leverage human capital resources.

- *Leadership assessment and development.* Leaders are the future of any business. An outsource partner must help define, assess, and identify potential leaders, managing their job assignments and career development to maximize their contributions to the organization.

- *Performance management.* Performance specialists should identify, communicate, and measure key performance indicators for specific job levels and individuals, linking employee evaluations and professional development plans to business goals.

REWARD AND INCENTIVIZE

Making sure that employees are working to full capacity requires a well-crafted reward and incentive program. This program must ensure that accurate and efficient management of employee benefits, compensation, and retirement plans is developed, delivered, and communicated effectively.

The right outsourcing partner will create a flexible, scalable model, customized to the organization's HR department, with a single contact for all employees and managers:

- *Health and welfare administration strategies.* Streamlined health and welfare benefits will facilitate the processes surrounding day-to-day benefits administration. These strategies should include employee benefits enrollment, vendor collaboration, and billing services.

- *Defined benefits outsourcing.* On an insourcing, outsourcing, or cosourcing basis, your vendor should provide a full range of pension plan administration, including database maintenance, pension statements, and compliance consulting.

- *Defined contribution administration.* Comprehensive services for 401(k), employee stock ownership plan (ESOP), and other defined contribution plans should offer convenience and flexibility without the limitations of bundled product, and should cover the two main areas of interest to any plan sponsor: administration and investment.

REDEPLOY AND RETIRE

When employees move on, their HR needs often become even more complex. Benefits related to termination, transfers, and retirement can be cumbersome and time-consuming, taking HR professionals away from business strategy.

A strategic outsourcing provider will provide end-to-end solutions that effectively cover this phase of an employee's tenure, including communication strategies, call center support, and combined investment administration to deliver comprehensive services related to the redeployment and retirement of the workforce:

- *Retiree processing and counseling.* This should include the full scope of employee retirement, including pension benefits calculations, benefits options communications, and retiree data tracking and maintenance.
- *Terminated employee processing.* Employee termination includes preparing termination papers, establishing eligibility for benefits and pension, administering COBRA, and managing discharged employees cases, including any legal proceedings that may arise.

- *Transfer and reorganization processing.* Employees who are transferred due to career or organizational changes have distinct needs. An effective outsourcing vendor will help administer and execute employee transfers, including employee records, payroll, and benefits records.

The Financial Executive's Perspective on HRO

As much as 80 percent of a company's worth is tied to its workforce. As the preceding section illustrates, making the most of human capital involves strategic recruiting, hiring, training, and retention programs that focus on bringing the best people into the organization, giving them the tools to ensure optimal performance, and keeping them satisfied through competitive compensation packages and career development opportunities.

Savvy financial executives at leading organizations are beginning to recognize the potentially enormous business benefits of HRO, knowing as they do that the market value of most companies today is only partially represented by physical assets, or those assets in the annual report. CFOs and controllers realize that human capital is the true differentiator in the marketplace, and the ability to maximize workforce performance to achieve business objectives is paramount to long-term success.

According to some financial experts, while stock share performance is often linked more closely to broader issues of market confidence, interest rates, industry performance, and accounting practices than the business fundamentals of an organization, it is in the long-term operational interests of all businesses to trim cost structures and enhance workforce performance. In recent surveys, financial analysts evaluating initial public offerings (IPOs) frequently cite HR-related issues, such as quality of staff and level of incentive pay tied to performance, as key factors contributing to potential investor interest and overall longevity following the IPO. Outperforming the industry and the stock market average helps organizations attract investors, improve shareholder value, and raise capital for further acquisitions or investments. The right HRO partner can work with business leaders to effectively align human capital to these core business objectives.

From a financial perspective, money spent on HR is an expense, and therefore HR spending immediately affects the organization's bottom line. This is in contrast to investments in hard assets, such as property, equipment, or technical systems, which depreciate over time, resulting in a weaker short-term effect. Many finance executives realize that the opportunity to better manage their resources can be found in focusing more strongly on workforce costs. The Financial Accounting Standards Board (FASB) and other professional organizations are working to improve the accounting of human assets, and several leading companies currently report on human capital in their annual reports. These trends have already begun and will continue to gain momentum in the coming years. The most strategic and successful finance professionals will lead their organizations in this direction, ahead of competitors.

Using Reverse Requests for Proposals to Build Stronger Outsourcing Relationships

In most outsourcing arrangements, the traditional means of evaluating a vendor is the request for proposal (RFP). Companies conduct an internal assessment to identify operational and transactional needs, develop an RFP, and submit it to a number of outsourcing vendors with the appropriate qualifications. Once a vendor is chosen and due diligence is completed, contract negotiations begin.

According to an article by HRO experts Jay F. Stright and Frank J. Candio, the RFP is no longer the recommended procedure for exploring outsourcing options. They say, "Beginning with an RFP limits too rigidly the 'box' into which solutions are going to fit. The RFP's predefinition often eliminates options that are the right ones for the customer. In a new and rapidly developing market, most organizations are not in a position to determine which flavor of outsourcing makes sense for them until they are well into the assessment process."

Using a reverse RFP approach is an alternative and improved option for finding the right outsourcing vendor and building stronger, more strategic, and more effective outsourcing relationships. In this approach, instead of sending out an RFP, the company collaborates with a select number of vendors, each with its own operating model and outsourcing methodology. The reverse RFP method gives the company a chance to see itself through the vendors' perspectives, creating the opportunity to adopt different points of view, philosophies, and styles before choosing one that fits its needs. In many cases, the company may modify its own business objectives and operating model to align with the outsourcer of its choice. In short, the reverse RFP approach can be a learning process for the company, one that may yield greater results than anticipated.

Typically, companies seek an HRO vendor to merely handle back-office functions. If a company is not looking for a deep HRO strategy, it will send out an RFP that is narrow and limiting in scope. As a result, the company may miss a significant opportunity to find an HRO partner prepared to optimize workforce value and build enterprisewide value.

The reverse RFP process has two key components. One is an internal feasibility study, conducted jointly by the potential outsourcing vendors and the company representatives. The purpose of the study is to develop a blueprint of the company's existing business environment, including operational infrastructure, IT systems, corporate culture, market pressures, competitor analysis, and strategic goals.

It is critical at this early stage that the potential HRO providers be given access to the internal operating environment of the company in order to gather as much information as possible and understand where improvements can be made, business processes streamlined, costs reduced, and workforce value maximized. Without this perspective, the HRO vendor can give only a generic recommendation for improvement, not a customized, value-adding one.

The second component is proactive collaboration between the outsourcing candidates and the company. In this stage, the HRO providers will outline the company's immediate needs, such as reducing head count, trimming costs, and reallocating HR resources. Additionally, the HRO providers can help sharpen the company's focus on key goals and objectives, and demonstrate how strategic outsourcing solutions can help meet those objectives. As discussed earlier, the right HRO partner can guide a company to improving its competitive advantage, not only by traditional means of reducing costs and increasing production, but by nontraditional methods—for example, by enhancing employee satisfaction through a stronger commitment to professional development and advancement programs.

That more and more companies are adopting the reverse
RFP approach is a signal to the HRO industry that it is on the
threshold of tremendous change. Savvy business leaders are
recognizing that HRO providers can and should be regarded
as strategic business partners, and that the stronger the relationship they build with those providers, the greater their return on outsourcing investments will be.

Can Campus Recruiting Really Be Effectively Outsourced?

Daniel Williams and John Flato

CEO and President, respectively, Elite Graduate Jobs

Many HR functions, transactional and strategic, are effectively outsourced to third-party vendors, including compensation planning and implementation, benefits administration, experienced hire recruiting, payroll, safety, security, reference checking, and so on. Organizations outsource so that they may concentrate their human capital and financial resources on their firms' key corporate competencies. As you have seen throughout this book, great companies are built by providing better, less expensive, and/or higher-quality products or services to their customers. They do not surpass the competition by building a non-revenue-generating overhead infrastructure, which has a long-term financial effect on the firm's bottom line in terms of salaries, benefits, pensions, and turnover.

In today's environment, nothing is "off the table" in terms of purchasing a service from a vendor who specializes in that function. In fact, some companies are outsourcing their own product or service, and are selling it with their own brand label. For example, accounting giant Ernst & Young outsources American tax filings to India to be completed by trained, but less expensive, accountants. Blue jeans makers, like Levi Strauss, no longer manufacture their products in the United States; they outsource or license the production of their jeans to companies abroad, where labor costs are a fraction of U.S. wages. Levi Strauss and others in the fashion industry have effectively become marketing companies, and not manufacturers.

In an Electronic Recruiting Exchange piece dated February 17, 2005, David Lefkow quoted an HR vice president who stated that "... it's my *fiduciary responsibility* to examine all possibilities" to save his company money. This is a far cry from years past, when HR vice presidents primarily thought about how to build a company organically. Cost savings initiatives were left for departments outside of HR. Now, heads of HR are asking themselves and their staffs, "What are my options to deliver better service at the lowest possible cost?" HR outsourcing guru, Tom Wimer of Knowledgebank, a northern Virginia–based HR outsourcing firm, says, "If the HR senior vice president is not evaluating HR outsourcing opportunities, or advising the CEO or board of directors of these cost-saving options, then s/he is not doing their job."

Daniel Williams, CEO of EliteGraduateJobs, saw a market need for outsourced college recruitment in the United Kingdom in the late 1990s. Oxbridgejobs, the U.K. forerunner to EliteGraduateJobs, carved a niche for itself in the recruitment market by providing high-caliber, well-screened candidates to companies whose own internal campus recruiting functions were struggling to keep pace with need during the dot-com boom.

The company attracted a client list that included some of the biggest names in the investment banking, consulting, and corporate world, as well as smaller firms that were expanding and had not yet established an infrastructure needed to hire from campuses.

John Flato is a college recruiting expert who ran the campus recruiting efforts in multiple industries, as well as serving as the career management director at Georgetown University's MBA program. He understands that college recruitment is a relationship business forged among colleges, universities, and companies. He also contends that this relationship can be built between third parties just as easily as the companies themselves.

Reasons to Outsource All or Parts of Your Campus Recruiting Effort

YOUR ANNUAL RECRUITING GOALS VARY, AND YOU DON'T WANT TO HIRE ADDITIONAL STAFF OR FIRE THEM

College recruiting is often a bellwether of the economy. When the economy is strong, campus recruiting needs are great. When there is a slowdown in the economy, campus goals are reduced. As a result, many companies that experience wide variances in their campus goals hire and lay off staff, or redeploy their college recruiting professionals from year to year. Outsourcing all or part of the campus recruiting effort may smooth out the peaks and valleys of hiring goals that most firms experience. Flato's former employer, Cap Gemini, a multinational consulting firm, is a prime example of the variability of the campus recruiting staff. At its peak in 1999, there were 45 people on staff devoted to campus recruiting. Today, Cap Gemini dedicates 1.5 full-time resources to that function. This is a common story, especially over the past decade, which has seen fluctuating economic fortunes in the economy as a whole, as well as extensive mergers and outsourcing trends, all of which changed the dynamic of HR as a whole. This point was magnified at the campus level, where hiring went from the frenzied levels of 1999 to a situation just two years later when major companies were reneging en masse on offers to candidates.

YOU HAVE NOT BEEN SUCCESSFUL ATTRACTING DIVERSE CANDIDATES

Many companies have difficulty attracting certain kinds of candidates, such as diverse candidates, or specialists, like IT professionals, whose function may fall outside of a firm's core competencies. Engaging a third-party firm to interface with diversity organizations or computer science and related technology departments, for example, can enable a firm to attract the quality of candidate and specialties that the firm needs, without additional costs of hiring specialized recruiting staff to perform those searches.

THE CANDIDATES YOU ATTRACT ARE CAPABLE OF DOING THE WORK, BUT DIDN'T TELL THE WHOLE TRUTH IN THE INTERVIEW

Students today are better trained in how to interview for a job than the interviewers are trained in evaluating the students' sincerity, motivation, and capabilities. Students are sophisticated enough to tell college recruitment professionals what they want to hear. For example, a student might tell an investment banker that he or she wants to be a banker. The next day, the same student might tell a large consultancy that he or she wants to be a management consultant, thus yielding offers from both. By working with a third-party recruiter that is truly assessing candidates and eliciting their lifelong goals, the third party can perform a better match between the students' true interests and the companies' needs. Daniel Williams calls it the "beyond the resume" assessment. Traditionally, companies have hired based on the strength of quantitative background matches—GPAs, SATs, degree, university, etc.—allied with interviews conducted with HR professionals and line managers. Essentially, hiring is geared toward finding candidates who are able, technically, to do a job. What a good third party will do is to find candidates who are ready, willing, and able to fill future management positions. Candidates who have the skill sets and backgrounds required, but who are also prepared for the work environment and who are genuinely interested in being a long-term employee of that company, are what companies seek.

College hires leave firms in droves within the first couple of years. Having a third-party interface enables a company to achieve closer matches of graduates' career choices and company positions.

YOUR COST PER HIRE (CPH) DOESN'T TELL THE WHOLE STORY

Although there have been many attempts to quantify cost per hire in the campus recruiting industry, there has not been one true standard, where *all* components of the recruiting process are captured. Those CPH measures that have been adopted do not always measure the soft costs of non-HR staff that participate in the recruiting process, that is, the prorated salary of non-HR professionals who are away from the office. Most companies calculate out-of-pocket expenses, like travel, merchandise, and advertising, but not the opportunity cost of the time non-HR employees take from their from primary responsibilities to participate in recruiting activities. For example, partners in law and consulting firms may actively participate in on-campus interviewing (e.g., student presentations and on-site interviews). Unfortunately, in the professional services field, time spent campus recruiting negatively impacts utilization (billable hours), a key metric used to measure compensation and bonuses and to determine which employees to retain when cutbacks are imminent. When belts tighten, consultants want to have the highest utilization possible. All this lost productivity is not captured in commonly used CPH metrics.

PEOPLE DON'T STAY IN CAMPUS RECRUITING POSITIONS FOREVER

Although it is recognized that campus recruiting is a relationship business, companies still experience voluntary and nonvoluntary turnover of their campus recruiting staffs. There are a number of reasons for campus recruiting staff leaving after one or two years. First, the recruiting periods are seasonal, with extensive peaks in the fall and spring. Second, it is grueling and tiring work that burns out the staff. Good college recruiters are constantly traveling from September to December, and then again from February to April, and communicating with applicants from their hotel rooms late into the evenings. After a couple of years on the road, campus recruiters tend to burn out, and with a change of staff all faculty and career management relationships are lost. Companies often reward good campus recruiters with other HR positions that will involve less travel and will expand their scope of responsibilities. Campus recruiting positions are, in turn, filled with young recently graduated employees, and these positions become a pass-through function. It is no surprise that the number-one complaint that career services professionals have with the companies that come to their campuses is that each year they are training a new cadre of recruiters on how to source candidates from their institutions. Rarely do they see the same people year to year.

YOU WANT TO CAST A WIDER NET

Companies usually have a core list of schools from which they recruit. Customarily, this list is kept small to maximize exposure with limited resources. As a result of limiting a firm's exposure to a few schools, the company is missing outstanding candidates from universities outside of the core. The use of a third party can cast a wider net by prescreening candidates from noncore schools, who may be better matches for the firm than those it currently sees. For example, students may bypass colleges of high academic standards for which they may be qualified and attend lesser-status universities for a variety of reasons, such as finances, proximity to family or job, or poor guidance counseling in high school. A third-party firm can assist companies to obtain high-quality candidates from noncore schools who are equally competitive with many of the candidates sourced from core schools, and who will bring a diversity of thought and perspective to the firm. If HR vice presidents look at the alma maters of their most successful employees, they no doubt will find that more than 50 percent of these schools are not on the core school recruiting list.

Components of Campus Recruiting that Can Be Outsourced Efficiently

BACK-ROOM OPERATIONS

Functions such as scheduling with universities, ensuring that recruiting materials like the schedules and brochures get to recruiters, working with vendors on campus so the right food and beverages arrive, and applicant tracking components, including negate letters, can be easily outsourced.

PRESCREENING OF CANDIDATES

Phone screens and/or psychometric testing can be used to see if there is a match with a company's culture and competencies before on-campus interviewing takes place.

VIDEO INTERVIEWEWS

This can be done in a synchronous (real-time, like a videoconference) or asynchronous manner, where the interview is stored on a server so that hiring managers can view interviews at their convenience, compare and contrast candidates, and e-mail the interview to other decision makers.

ON-CAMPUS OR OTHER FACE-TO-FACE INTERVIEWS

Third-party recruiters can conduct on-campus interviews for clients. Some will come in their own name, but most will come on campus as representatives of the client firm, identifying themselves with the firm and even using a business card of that firm. Either method can work as long as recruiters are honest throughout the process, conveying to students and the career management staff that they are representing multiple companies.

What Types of Firms Can Benefit Most from College Recruitment Outsourcing?

1. Large companies that have well-developed college recruitment programs with staff and infrastructure and a consistent level of campus hires year to year, but they:

   - Need support in a specific area—in a particular service line or in a department that is not a part of the company's core functions. For example, a major bank might seek college recruitment support for its IT department, which hires college students but not with the same level of sophistication as the rest of the firm's departments.

   - Require assistance in a particular student niche, for example, sourcing diverse candidates.

   - Want to extend their reach to schools where they don't customarily recruit but from which they would welcome top-tier candidates.

2. Midsize companies that may have a small staff of college recruitment professionals to conduct all college recruiting efforts. An outsourced partner can provide a great level of support to augment an existing program.

3. Small to midsize companies that wish to employ campus hires, but the number of students they hire on an annual basis is inconsistent. In such cases, a dedicated college recruiting department is not necessary and outsourcing is a logical choice.

OUTSOURCING

Compared to the recent past, companies are being held to a much higher standard by stockholders, regulating agencies, and other stakeholders. Legislation has been passed that makes firms and their executives much more accountable. No longer can executives say that they do not fully understand significant transactions or approve certain expenditures. Vice presidents of HR now have much more exposure to and accountability to the firms' boards of advisers. Senior executives must look for every opportunity to maximize shareholder value, even if it means reducing head count and dismantling some departments.

Like other internal HR functions, outsourcing all or part of campus recruiting can be beneficial. There must be an internal champion, like a campus recruiting manager or director, who serves as a conduit to the lines of business and helps to facilitate the final stages of the hiring process. It has been proven that companies can reduce costs, find better talent that is more suitable for the firm, and become more efficient by using an outsourced partner with the expertise to successfully source, evaluate, and process new hires in a smooth and efficient manner.

A Strategic Approach to Outsourcing

Christopher J. Damm

Principal, Advent Health Technology

To achieve its objectives, a firm can choose to use its own resources or, through contracts and markets, those of other firms. Although it is possible to make such decisions based purely on near-term cost considerations, over the preceding century the choice between owning and buying productive capabilities has become increasingly strategic. Specifically, firms have used outsourcing to gain competitive advantage by assigning increasingly complex and fundamental tasks to specialized contractors. The arrangement has not always been successful, however, possibly because strategic outsourcing is complex, uncertain, or both.

The work presented here is designed to support managers in their quest to craft durable and profitable outsourcing decisions. We begin by examining outsourcing from a theoretical perspective, borrowing concepts from agent-principal theory, game theory, neoclassical economics, transaction cost economics, and the resource-based view of the firm. Although we will recognize academic traditions, our main purpose is integrative and practical. Using this foundation, we then will propose an algorithm for making informed and theoretically sound decisions about outsourcing.

Theoretical Overview

NEOCLASSICAL FOUNDATIONS

The modern theory of the firm, at least implicitly, begins with neoclassical economics. Representative works by Clark (1908), Knight (1921), and Marshall (1920) define the school that views the firm as an island of planned coordination in a market system predominantly governed by supply, demand, and price. Despite the passage of time, the theory still forms the core of modern managerial economics. Williamson (1996) observes,

> The basic theory of the firm that is featured in microeconomics textbooks describes the firm in technological terms as a "production function" in which inputs (labor, capital) are transformed into outputs (goods, service) according to the laws of technology. Upon assigning an objective function to the firm (usually profit maximization) and describing the market in which it operates, students learn how firms set price and output and respond to changing opportunities (demand, input prices). (Williamson 1996, 131)

Although neoclassical theory does explain the operation of competitive and monopolistic markets, it leaves managers with a fairly limited set of options for creating profit. Firms can vary current output and long-term capital investment to maximize profits based on a known cost function and market prices. Suc-

cess will enable the firm to earn monopoly rents or, in competitive markets, an economic profit of zero. The firm also can attempt to improve underlying production technology to earn
Ricardian rents.

TRANSACTION COST ECONOMICS

Basic Framework In 1937, R. H. Coase addressed these limitations in a paper that defined transaction cost economics. In
considering the neoclassical view, Coase noted that the theory
leads to a clear demarcation between firms and their input
markets:

> Outside the firm, price movements direct production, which is
> coordinated through a series of exchange transactions on the
> market. Within a firm, these market transactions are eliminated
> and in place of the complicated market structure with exchange
> transaction is substituted the entrepreneur coordinator, who di-
> rects production. (Coase 1937)

Coase also noted, however, that, although the boundary was
clearly defined at any moment, it was dynamic over time as
managers optimized the balance between market transactions
outside the firm and the hierarchies that defined internal governance. He asserted that "the operation of a market costs something and by forming an organization and allowing some
authority (an entrepreneur) to direct the resources, certain marketing costs are saved" (392). This view implies an additional
role for the managers of firms:

> The question always is, will it pay to bring an extra exchange
> transaction under the organizing authority? At the margin, the

costs of organizing within the firm will be equal either to the costs of organizing in another firm or to the costs involved in leaving the transaction to be "organized" by the price mechanism. Businessmen will be constantly experimenting, controlling more or less and, in this way, equilibrium will be maintained. (403)

Although one might be tempted to categorize this approach as another method for improving production technology, its thrust seems both strategic and normative. By implication, managers who control the *boundaries* of their firms will gain profits that elude others, without any fundamental change in technology per se.

From this beginning, transaction cost economics has evolved in several ways. It has replaced an emphasis on hierarchical firms surrounded by perfect markets with an emphasis on flawed markets (Williamson 1996, 88) and hybrid modes of governance (Williamson 1988, 73). It explicitly recognizes intertemporal problems in contracting that are absent in neoclassical spot markets (Williamson 1988, 71). Finally, it examines additional contractual hazards related to the assignment of residual property rights (Grossman and Hart 1986). Overall, the current approach can be summarized as follows:

The basic hypothesis out of which transaction cost economics works is that of discriminating alignment: transactions, which differ in their attributes, align with governance structures, which differ in their cost and competence, so as to effect a transaction cost economizing outcome. (Williamson 1996, 138)

For transactions that occur outside the bounds of neoclassical economics, contracts are the typical governance structure that "should be thought of as a triple in which price, the attributes of the transaction, and contractual safeguards are all determined simultaneously. The latter two are transaction cost economic supplements to the more familiar neoclassical concept of contract as mediated by price" (Williamson 1996, 139).

Canonical Problems   Both aficionados and critics have suggested that transaction cost theory could be tautological (Williamson 1988, 65), and that "almost anything can be rationalized by invoking suitable specified transaction costs" (Fisher 1977, 5, cited in Williamson 1988, 65). Practical application, however, is facilitated by consideration of the two canonical problems of transaction cost economics: incomplete contracts and investment in specific assets.

Incomplete Contracts   Transaction cost economics is based on two foundational behavioral assumptions: bounded rationality and opportunism. Bounded rationality, "the inability of the human mind to find or process all the information about a transaction" (Aubert 2004) results in uncertainty and the inevitability of incomplete contracts in which the parties cannot foresee, much less control, *ex post* contingencies. Hart and Moore (1999) provide a simple parable that has been subject to substantial analysis:

> Imagine a buyer, B, who requires a good (or service) from a seller, S. Suppose that the exact nature of the good is uncertain; more precisely, it depends on a state of nature which is yet to be realized. In an ideal world, the parties would write a contingent contract specifying exactly which good is to be delivered in each state. However, if the number of states is very large, such a contract would be prohibitively expensive. So instead, the parties

will write an incomplete contract. Then, when the state of nature is realized, they will renegotiate the contract, since at this stage they know what kind of good should be traded. (115)

In addition to bounded rationality, opportunism is embedded in this problem. Williamson (1988) writes that opportunism "is a deep condition of self-interest seeking that contemplates guile. Promises to behave responsibly that are unsupported by credible commitments will not, therefore, be reliably discharged" (68). One might imagine, in this Hobbesian "state of nature," that hazards other than uncertainty flow from incomplete contracts as parties use *ex ante* information and *ex post* governance costs to their individual advantage.

Analysis of even simple incomplete contracts is complex,[1] but several themes emerge that are illustrated by relatively accessible analysis by Hart and Moore (1999). Their specification of the problem includes the following:

At date 0, a buyer and a seller contract for the sale of a "special" widget that can either be described without cost (D) or is prohibitively expensive to describe (ND).

At date _____, the seller invests in manufacture, with $\int$ denoting an optimal investment that results in the best outcome for all parties.

At date 1, the parties trade based on an offer by the seller, with a provision for renegotiation (R+) if the buyer rejects the offer or (R–) if renegotiation is not possible.

---

[1]See Fudenberg and Tirole (1990), Hart and Moore (1999), Hermalin and Katz (1991), Ishiguro and Ito (2001), Ma (1988), Maskin and Tirole (1999), and Matthews (1995).

Their principal findings are:

R– cases lead to a best outcome for the parties.

The seller will invest $\int$ at date _____, and set a price for the buyer that reflects whether the final widget is indeed special or generic. The buyer will pay the full value of the special widget, because delivery from an alternate vendor would be uncertain.

R+ cases favor the buyer, producing a generic outcome.

At date 1, buyer will refuse the special price and bargain to level of seller's best alternative price, possibly extracting the entire surplus. Knowing this, the seller will never invest in manufacture of the special widget.

D/ND factors appear not to matter, as R+ or R– factors dominate. In practical terms, however, an R– contract is difficult to create.

Insurance, middlemen, and replacement contracts can undermine both initial contracts and third-party referees.

Reallocation of property rights can help when contracts are incomplete.

Downstream integration, through asset ownership, can change the seller's incentives. This applies both to complete ownership and to joint ventures.

Even so, the possibility of joint ownership does not necessarily produce robust solutions.

Although it is difficult to translate the closed-form solutions of simple models directly into practice, the results of these analyses provide insight into the basic parameters of outsourcing decisions. Some of these are counterintuitive.

High litigation costs, as undesirable as they may seem, may help deter renegotiation where they are comparable in magnitude to contract value. Uncertainty about the qualities of the widget in question potentially are less important than whether price negotiations are possible on delivery.

Specific Assets   Asset specificity can be defined by the difference between the cost of an asset and the value of its next best use (Williamson 1981, 1547). In a bilateral relationship without adequate contractual protection, investment in specific assets by one party can allow the noninvesting party to extract all or part of the value of the investment. The investor is subject to so-called lock-in because its alternative to exploitation by the counterparty is an even greater loss by employing the asset its next best use. Without uncertainty, it may be possible to mitigate investments by either creating a mutual hostage arrangement or dual sourcing (Bahli and Rivard 2003, 213). The parties can take each other hostage either through joint investment in the specific assets or through allocation of downstream payments or profits. The Japanese system of *keiretsu*, for example, may be the result of the specific assets investments required to create a tightly integrated supply chain. Dual or multiple sourcing allows the investing party potentially to walk away from lock-in attempts, though one might imagine that this would work only in situations where (1) collusion is not possible and (2) the opportunistic party would incur costs as a result of contract termination.

From a practical standpoint, managers negotiating outsourcing arrangements should carefully track investments in specific assets and, where necessary, devise joint ownership schemes to protect their interests.

AGENT-PRINCIPAL THEORY

Although the works of Hart and Moore (1999) and Maskin and Tirole (1999) can be considered examples of agent-principal theory, there is additional work in the field that has not been incorporated into transaction cost economics. Perhaps the most accessible of this is Zhou's graphical approach to the standard agent-principal model (Holstrom 1979). His work covers a one-period contract where the agent's production curve is uncertain and convex in effort and his cost and utility functions are concave.[2] The agent's pay is linear with fixed ($\langle$) and incentive ((R)) components. This model, with our interpretations incorporated, yields several insights:

> Without uncertainty (or for a risk-neutral agent), the agent will prefer 100 percent incentive pay with no fixed component. Overall, this also yields the best solution for all parties.
>
> Not surprisingly, with increasing uncertainty (or risk aversion) $\langle$ will rise as the agent requires insurance against uncertainty.
>
> More interestingly, due to the shape of the *feasible* cost curve,[3] any given $\langle$ will be associated with two values for (R). In one case, decreasing incentive payments will be associated with increasing $\langle$, a trade-off of risk and reward as one might expect. In the second, $\langle$ and (R) will decrease in

---

[2]These are all fairly standard production assumptions and could be represented using Cobb-Douglas production functions and quadratic utility.
[3]Here determined by zero expected economic profit and compatibility with structure of incentive payments.

tandem, suggesting without adequate insurance, the agent will move toward abandoning a risky project altogether (⟨ and (R) = 0).

In a given transaction, it would be difficult to determine if an agent is choosing a low-effort or a high-effort combination. In a situation where a principal can choose among several agents, it might consider allowing each agent to choose its own combination of insurance and incentive payments. Bids should then be judged based on predicted total cost and the portion of total cost allocated to incentive payments. The foregoing analysis suggests that the bids of motivated and efficient agents should form an efficient frontier that minimizes ⟨ while maximizing (R).

RESOURCE-BASED VIEW

Thus far, we have used transaction cost economics and its related disciplines in order to create a view of interactions between firms that is far richer than the neoclassical reliance on price alone. Here we will summarize the resource-based view (RBV) of the firm, which illuminates the inner workings of the neoclassical "black box" firm. The RBV rejects the concept of the firm as a simple mathematical function based on cost, price, and demand, and posits that an industry's firms are a heterogeneous collection of productive resources. Although market power might explain profit, differences among firms are equally important.

Devotees of the RBV have been active for more than 40 years. The citations of most active scholars suggest that Edith Penrose is the founding mother of the school. Here is her articulation of the RBV (1959):

A firm is more than an administrative unit; it is also a collection of productive resources the disposal of which between different uses over time is determined by administrative decision. (30)[4]

Strictly speaking, it is never resources themselves that are the "inputs" in the production process, but only the services that the resources can render. (31)

The important distinction between resources and services is not their relative durability; rather it lies in the fact that resources consist of a bundle of potential services and can, for the most part, be defined independently of their use, while services cannot be so defined, the very word "service" implying a function, an activity. As we shall see, it is largely in this distinction that we find the source of the uniqueness of each individual firm. (31)

Variations and extensions of this approach have occupied economists since its publication, but the central themes of the school have remained constant. Consider, for example, these points by Prahalad and Hamel (1990):

Core competencies are the collective learning in the organization, especially how to coordinate diverse production skills and integrate multiple streams of technologies. (82)

In the long run, competitiveness derives from an ability to build, at lower cost and more speedily than competitors, the core competencies that spawn unanticipated products. The real sources of advantage are to be found in management's ability to consolidate corporatewide [sic] technologies and production skills into competencies that empower individual business to adapt quickly to changing opportunities. (81)

---

[4]Page numbers refer a reprinted version of the Penrose (1959) in Foss (1997), which is an excellent anthology of articles related to the RBV.

Here *technologies* and *production skills* are clearly analogous to Penrose's *resources* and *services*.[5] Applying similar parsimony to other explicators and proponents of the RBV, the following appear to be its central themes:[6]

A firm's *capabilities* stem from its underlying *resources*.

Resources are bound to the firm through *isolating mechanisms*, resulting in sustainable rents and/or competitive advantage.

Firms in a given industry are *heterogeneous* with respect to their resources and capabilities.

The following sections will expand these points, based on the work of a number of authors and editors (Barney 1991, Dierickx and Cool 1989, Foss 1997, Peteraf 1993, Prahalad and Hamel 1990, Rumelt 1987, Teece et al., 1997 and Wernerfelt 1984).

Resources and Capabilities   Resources can be tangible or intangible and capabilities can be manifest or latent. Most authors also emphasize that resources are distinct from a firm's physical assets. For example, one could consider Merck's scientists and their culture of discovery as a key resource of the firm. Their current deployment gives the company the capability to discover drugs that define new therapeutic areas and to clear regulatory barriers more efficiently than competitors. This enables the firm to produce products and earn rents at or above the cost

---

[5]If only *we* could borrow so shamelessly!

[6]This structure of this summary owes much to the editorial choices by Foss (1997) and a recap of the literature by Peteraf (1993).

of capital (Sender 1994). Although some authors identify patents as resources, this assertion seems to miss the hierarchical spirit of the argument.[7] Patents are obviously valuable, but the resources that produce them efficiently are perhaps more fundamental to the firm.

"The routine component of strategy formulation is the constant search for ways in which the firm's unique resources can be redeployed in changing circumstances" (Rumelt 1984 in Foss 1997, 142). In cases where capabilities and resources are tangible, evolving strategies are sometimes clear. Sony managers, for example, probably had little difficulty in deciding to apply the firm's miniaturization capabilities to successive generations of portable tape players. The redeployment of intangible resources, however, is less straightforward.

Disney World runs, in part, based on the cohesive and conformist culture of its employees. Attempted deployment of this resource, however, using French employees at Euro Disney was not successful by most accounts.

The fact that resources can be "tacit or socially complex" (Peteraf 1993, 184) is not the only obstacle to strategic management. Relationships between resources, capabilities, and firm performance are often characterized by "causal ambiguity" (Rumelt 1984 in Foss 1997, 135).

Isolating Mechanisms   Perhaps the most important component of the RBV is its focus on isolating mechanisms, a term originally used by Rumelt (1984) to refer to "phenomena which

---

[7]This hierarchical approach is very much in the spirit of both Penrose (1959) and Prahalad and Hamel (1990).

protect individual forms from imitation and preserve their rent streams" (Peteraf 1993, 182). These include:

Causal ambiguity.

Imperfect mobility.

Path dependence.

Causal ambiguity, first described by Lippman and Rumelt (1982), interferes with competitors' ability to create "carbon copies" of successful firms. Such "uncertain imitability" can be expressed in statistical terms and, in itself, can be a source of rent.[8] (Given that it can also be a source of confusion for a firm's own strategic managers, however, it is perhaps not a preferred mode of rent production.)

Imperfect mobility, which refers to the inability to separate resources from the firm, sustains rent-producing resources within the firm (Peteraf 1994, 186). Favorable location or cheek-by-jowl production requirements (blast furnace, rolling mill) are tangible examples of imperfect mobility. More subtle examples include supplier relationships that depend on employee culture and tacit knowledge. Some authors suggest that imperfect mobility is present when an asset is nontradable.

Path dependence is also an important isolating mechanism. Dierickx and Cool (1989), for example, describe path dependence as part of the process of "asset stock accumulation":

A key dimension of strategy formulation may be identified as the task of making appropriate choices about strategic expenditures (advertising spending, R&D outlays, etc.) with a view to accu-

---

[8]See Rumelt (1984) for a closed-form solution.

mulating required resources and skills (brand loyalty, technological expertise, etc.). In other words, appropriate time paths of relevant flow variables must be chosen to build required asset
stocks. Critical or strategic asset stocks are those assets which are
nontradeable . . . nonimitable, and nonsubstitutable. (1506–1507)

To paraphrase, the creation of privileged resource positions
depends on both time and choice. According to the authors, such
path dependence interferes with imitation through time com-
pression diseconomies, asset mass efficiencies, interconnected-
ness of asset stocks, and causal ambiguity (1989, 1507–1510).

Heterogeneity "A basic assumption of resource-based work is
that the resource bundles and capabilities underlying production are heterogeneous across firms" (Peteraf 1992, 180). This
may represent the capture of scarce resources to produce Ricardian rents, the attainment of market power through monopoly,
a divergent response to an ambiguous competitive environment
(Rumelt 1984 in Foss 1997), or path-dependent evolution of the
firm (Dierickx and Cool 1989).

Implications for Outsourcing Overall, the RBV suggests that:

Fundamental resources should not be considered for outsourcing, because the strategic imperative is continued asset
stock accumulation.

Connections between resources, which may not be readily
apparent, mean that even generic functions might require the
support of the firm's resource environment.

Cultural dimensions within the firm might be crucial in mold-
ing performance to customer expectations—inviting degrada-
tion of products and services if managers use outsourcing.

Spinout of divisions or training of providers outside the firm could accelerate imitation by competitors.

The existence of heterogeneity suggests that pack behavior with regard to outsourcing decisions is potentially dangerous.

Strategic Outsourcing in Practice

OVERVIEW

The foregoing theoretical summary suggests that any outsourcing decision should be subject to a complex array of considerations and tests. Unfortunately, despite our attempts to create a sparse taxonomy of terminology and principles, it is not immediately apparent how real firms might use the literature to improve outsourcing decisions. Because that is our overall goal, we now turn our attention from theory to implementation.

We imagine a situation where a team leader, familiar with both the theory and her firm, leads a group of company analysts in a process that has two phases. First, the group undertakes an analysis of the firm that reveals the firm's resources and capabilities. Second, the group makes an audit of its proposed outsourcing decisions using concepts from transaction cost economics and agent-principal theory.

ANALYSIS

One potential method for revealing a firm's capabilities and resources is the "activity map" proposed by Porter (1996). The finished maps consist of a network of light yellow and dark purple circles connected by heavy and light lines. Inside each circle are the "tailored activities" that the company uses to underwrite its strategy. When complete,

> Activity maps ... show how a company's strategic position is contained within a set of tailored activities designed to deliver it. In companies with a clear strategic position, a number of higher-order strategic themes (in dark purple) can be identified and implemented through clusters of tightly linked activities (in light yellow). (71)

Ikea's activity map, for example, contains 20 circles, Vanguard's twenty-three. Southwest Airlines' activity system is included on the facing page. Connections between activities demonstrate fit with overall strategy. Porter continues:

> Activity system maps can be useful for examining and strengthening strategic fit. A set of basic questions should guide the process. First, is each activity consistent with the overall positioning—the varieties produced, the need served, and the type of customers accessed? Ask those responsible for each activity to identify how other activities within the company improve or detract from their performance. Second, are there ways to strengthen how activities and groups of activities reinforce one another? Finally, could changes in one activity eliminate the need to perform others? (72)

Bold lines indicate the connections between the company's most important activities.

Cynics might dismiss this as so much consulting hoodoo. We would disagree for several reasons:

> The RBV suggests that any activity that is a candidate for outsourcing might have a critical relationship to the firm's key

resources, through either its direct interconnections or its effect on asset stock accumulation.[9]

Bounded rationality and causal ambiguity suggest that the nature of the connections between activities should be examined by those responsible for each activity as well as those affected by the activity.

Defining feedback loops of connections could illuminate problems in measuring performance by agents or identify the appropriate point of monitoring agency within the organization.

Overall, Porter's approach is an appealing attempt to inject systems thinking into corporate strategic planning.[10]

One might improve Porter's approach in two ways.[11] First, the lines connecting activities should indicate the frequency and complexity of the communication between activities. Accompanying documentation should also define the connection more explicitly.

Second, the maps should be subject to a secondary analysis that links activities to the underlying resources and capabilities that support them. This could be accomplished by tagging individual activities with letters or colors. With these illuminated maps, the team should be ready to audit potential outsourcing decisions.

AUDIT

The audit begins by identifying activities that are candidates for outsourcing. Based on Porter's criteria, the team then determines

---

[9]Sometimes valuable concepts are worth their "verbal diseconomies."
[10]See Senge (1990) for a broader discussion of business systems analysis.
[11]This argument is motivated by the principles of object-oriented design and analysis. See Booch (1994) for an overview.

if any of the activities are "higher-order strategic themes" that are closely related to the company's competitive position. If so, they are unlikely to be candidates for outsourcing. Conversely, activities that are peripherally connected to the company's strategic position and that are available through competitive markets should be strongly considered for outsourcing.

Next, informed by the RBV, the team asks the following questions:

How closely is the activity linked to the company's underlying resources and capabilities?

Does the company perform the activity with superior quality or efficiency because of a connection with an underlying resource or capability?

Does the activity improve or augment the company's capabilities resources in any way?

Would outsourcing require extensive interaction between vendors and activities that represent the company's unique capabilities and resources?

What is the frequency and quality of the interactions between this activity and others in the organization?

These questions are designed to uncover whether activities are representative of the company's unique resources and whether they enhance asset stock accumulation. Further, the limitation of interaction between the company's key resources and external agents is designed to support other isolating mechanisms. Finally, activities that are characterized by frequent and intimate interactions within the firm are likely to be supported by both tacit knowledge and cultural norms. It would be difficult to support such activities outside the firm.

OUTSOURCING

Next, informed by transaction cost economics, the team asks the following questions:

Is the activity available on a spot market or will it be governed by an incomplete contract?

Are specific asset investments involved?

What is the timing of investments by each party?

Are there barriers to renegotiation?

Clearly, the best candidates for outsourcing are services that are available on competitive spot markets. Governance consists only of price, and a firm not dedicated to these markets is unlikely to do as well as those that are. Remedies for specific asset investments were described earlier and include ownership of residual property rights and mutual hostaging. From the standpoint of the outsourcing firm, models of incomplete contracts also suggest that renegotiation at the time of delivery of services or goods is desirable, because it allows buyers to capture the surplus in a bilateral incomplete contract.

Several additional questions could alert the team to potential agent-principal problems:

When and how can the value of the outsourced product be measured?

Can the effort expended by the agent be easily measured?

How uncertain is the relationship between the agent's effort and his desired outcome?

Delays and uncertainty in measurement are the basis for agent-principal problems. Perhaps less intuitive is the finding that uncertainty in outcome will lead the agent to make choices in effort that are not in the company's interest, even in the setting of a negotiated combination of fixed and incentive payments. As described earlier, bidding in both fixed and incentive payments may be able to separate high-effort from low-effort agents.

Of course, managers considering outsourcing decisions might also find traditional make-buy calculations useful in the limited number of situations where they believe that they can effectively compete with suppliers operating in competitive input factor markets.

In practice, it probably would be wise to supplement the questions suggested here with role-playing exercises. Although the problems in the theoretical literature clearly define parameters that should concern managers, they also include assumptions and inputs that are difficult to verify in real-world situations. Even the theorists recognize the limitations.

Rumelt (1984) observes:

> Because strategic opportunities are by definition uncertain and connected to the possession of unique information or resources, strategic analysis must be situational. Just as there is no algorithm for creating wealth, strategic prescriptions that apply to broad classes of firms can only aid in avoiding mistakes, not in attaining advantage. (in Foss 1997, 143)

Williamson (1988 and 1996) also emphasizes that calculation of transaction costs involves detailed consideration of process and nanoeconomic factors that cannot be readily captured by a general theory.

Conclusions

The work presented here suggests that a strategic approach to outsourcing is both necessary and practical. Simple make-buy decisions, based on cost considerations alone, do not capture many of the risks involved in outsourcing. Although the theory that informs strategic outsourcing is not especially accessible, it can be made operational without either extraordinary effort or excessive dilution.

Several extensions of the concepts here would be interesting. First, it would be interesting to analyze formally bidding games that could improve the selection of agents described by the standard agent-principal problem. Second, application of the outsourcing algorithm presented here to cases such as Dell, long-term military contracting, and the IBM decision to outsource DOS to Microsoft would provide additional insight into its utility, or lack thereof. Third, actual tests of the method would undoubtedly reveal flaws and opportunities for improvement.

References

Aubert, B. A., S. Rivard, and M. Patry. 1996. A transaction cost approach to outsourcing behavior: Some empirical evidence. *Information & Management* 30(2):51–64.

Bahli, B., and S. Rivard. 2003. The information technology outsourcing risk: A transaction cost and agency theory-based perspective. *Journal of Information Technology* 18:211–221.

Barney, J. B. 1991. Firm resources and sustained competitive advantage. *Journal of Management* 42:99–120.

Booch, G. 1994. *Object-oriented analysis and design with applications*. Reading, MA: Addison-Wesley.

Clark, J. B. 1908. *The distribution of wealth*. New York: Macmillan Company. Library of Economics and Liberty.

Coase, R. H. 1937. The nature of the firm. *Economics N. S.* 4:386–405.

Dierickx, I., and K. Cool. 1989. Asset stock accumulation and sustainability of competitive advantage. *Management Science* 35:1504–1511.

Fisher, S. 1977. Long-term contracting, sticky prices, and monetary policy: Comment. *Journal of Monetary Economics* 3:317–324.

Grossman, S., and O. Hart. 1986. The costs and benefits of ownership: A theory of vertical and lateral integration. *Journal of Political Economy* 94(4):691–719.

Hart, O., and J. Moore. 1999. Foundations of incomplete contracts. *Review of Economic Studies* 66:115–138.

Foss, N., ed. 1997. *Resources, firms, and strategies: A reader in the resource-based perspective.* New York: Oxford University Press.

Fudenberg, D., and J. Triole. 1990. Moral hazard and renegotiation in agency contracts. *Econometrica* 58:1279–1320.

Hermalin, B. E., and M. L. Katz. 1991. Moral hazard and verifiability: The effects of renegotiation in agency. *Econometrica* 59:1735–1753.

Holstrom, B. 1979. Moral hazard and observability. *Bell Journal of Economics* 10(1):74–91.

Ishiguro, S., and H. Ito. 2001. Moral hazard and renegotiation with multiple agents. *Review of Economic Studies* 68:1–20.

Knight, F. H. 1921. *Risk, uncertainty, and profit.* Boston: Houghton Mifflin.

Lippman, S. A., and R. P. Rumelt. 1982. Uncertain imitability: An analysis of interfirm differences in efficiency under competition. *Bell Journal of Economics* 13:418–438.

Ma, A. C.-T. 1988. Renegotiation and optimality in agency contracts. *Review of Economic Studies* 61:109–129.

Marshall, A. 1920. *Principles of economics.* London: Macmillan and Co., Ltd.

Maskin, E., and J. Tirole. 1999. Unforeseen contingencies and incomplete contracts. *Review of Economic Studies* 66:83–114.

Matthews, S. A. 1995. Renegotiation of sales contracts. *Econometrica* 63:567–589.

Penrose, E. T. 1959. *The theory of the growth of the firm.* New York: John Wiley & Sons.

Peteraf, M. A. 1993. The cornerstones of competitive advantage: A resource-based view. *Strategic Management Journal*, 14:179–188.

Porter, M. E. 1996. What is strategy? *Harvard Business Review* 74(6):61–78.

Prahalad, C. K., and G. Hamel. 1990. The core competence of the corporation. *Harvard Business Review* 66:79–91.

Rumelt, R. P. 1987. Theory, strategy and entrepreneurship. *The Competitive Challenge.* Ed. David J. Teece. New York: Harper & Row, 137–158.

Sender, G. 1994. Option analysis at Merck. *Harvard Business Review* 72(1):92.

Senge, P. M. 1990. *The fifth discipline: The art and practice of the learning organization.* New York: Doubleday.

Teece, D. J., G. Pisano, and A. Shuen. 1997. Dynamic capabilities and strategic management. *Strategic Management Journal* 18:7.

Weintraub, E. R. 2004. Neoclassical economics. *The Concise Encyclopedia of Economics.* Liberty Fund, Inc. Ed. David R. Henderson. www.econlib.org/library/Enc/NeoclassicalEconomics.html, December 15, 2004.

Wernerfelt, B. 1984. A resource-based view of the firm. *Strategic Management Journal* 5:171–180.

Williamson, O. E. 1981. The modern corporation: Origins, evolution, attributes. *Journal of Economic Literature* 19(4):1537–1568.

Williamson, O. E. 1988. The logic of economic organization. *Journal of Law, Economics, and Organization* 4(1):65–93.

Williamson, O. E. 1996. Economics and organization: A primer. *California Management Review* 38(2):131–146.

Economics of Outsourcing

Gordon Walker
General Manager, Knowles Electronics

In 1937, Ronald Coase famously asked a fundamental question: Why do firms exist? More completely, why do transactions take place sometimes through a market and sometimes through internal organization within a firm? Forty years later, he almost as famously commented that although much was made of his query, very little was done with it.

Over the past 20+ years, quite a lot has been written in the fields of economics, management science, and strategy to address Coase's question both directly and indirectly. This paper will survey the landmark frameworks and concepts of these fields, and attempt to develop some insights into the underlying question of economic organization by applying the most relevant constructs to three business cases:

1. Knowles Electronics outsources, then insources, a critical component of its hearing-aid microphones.

2. JP Morgan Chase signs a landmark $5 billion, seven-year outsourcing pact with IBM in December 2002, and terminates it in September 2004 in favor of internal organization.

3. Knowles Electronics spends two years developing two outsourced suppliers of stamped metal parts, and then abandons commercial relations with both firms in February 2004 to set up its own operation in Malaysia.

All three cases deal with what management calls "vertical integration," or more uniquely "vertical reintegration" or "insourcing." Other monikers the press fits to these activities include "make vs. buy," "strategic sourcing," and assessment of "core competencies" leveraging "strategic assets." The literature is rich with academics and authors cum would-be consultants sharing their views on the subject.

This paper is organized as follows: The first section will cover the major topics in economics, from Coase's 1937 paper through the development and empirical testing of transactions cost economics and property rights theory. The next section surveys the management literature, borrowing heavily from the automotive sectors' make vs. buy literature and analysis utilizing systems engineering frameworks and developing a verbal argument around "dynamic instability" in organizational structures within an industry. The next section reviews key topics in strategy, from means of recognizing core competencies to strategic industry analysis and development of strategic assets. The final section breaks down the business cases already mentioned.

Economic Literature

THEORY OF THE FIRM

Coase's insight in 1937 was twofold: the organization of transactions through the market is not without cost, and firms incur costs to coordinate and organize activity internally. He identified a handful of likely sources of cost in using a market price mechanism. The first is the cost of discovering the price, which in some cases may be mediated by specialists or market-makers that effectively sell the information. Another cost might be in developing/negotiating the contract itself for the transaction, which is avoided but not eliminated in internal organization. On the costs of internal organization, Coase recognized that an ever-expanding firm would be increasingly difficult to coordinate, and that costs from managing such an organization would outweigh the benefits of avoiding the market transaction.

Oliver Williamson (1971) took up Coase's inquiry in the context of vertical integration and transaction costs. First, he asked why, if operating in competitive markets is costless, would anyone ever integrate? One answer is that not all markets are efficient. He also intuited that firms exist for a better reason than simple efficiency in scale or scope of work, that there is some benefit from the coordinating potential of an organization. He argued that internal organization will arise for transactional failures, when markets fail to work well, a condition met when markets function with nonmonopolistic pricing and low transaction costs are able to exploit available economies and provide for an acceptable risk premium.

Alchian and Demsetz (1972) took issue with the notion that firms avoid transaction costs in their ability to settle by fiat, rather than incur litigation, which had been a principle of the costly contracting argument. They recognized that a firm is simply an agglomeration of individual contracts with the firms' owner(s), and that the power of fiat extended only so far as those contracts stipulated or could be terminated. The conditions they viewed as necessary for the formulation of a firm were (1) increased productivity from cooperation, that the output of the firm would be more than the sum of the inputs, and (2) information effects, that the pooled activities could be more economically observed and rewards metered than in entrepreneurial contracting situations.

These works run very much in parallel, and combine to form some underlying structures and conditions upon which the further study of economic organization is based. The next subsection deals explicitly with the three principal elements.

ECONOMIC FOUNDATIONS

There is quite a lot written about the behaviors of industries and firms, and an almost wholly separate literature on the behaviors of individuals. Williamson's 1973 paper addressed the bridge— his so-called "human factors" in economic organization (EO) analysis—setting up two of the three elements that serve as the foundations for economic analysis.

The first assumption we make about the economic agents in our firms is what Williamson called "bounded rationality." This is the notion that individuals are limited in their ability and capacity to store and process information. Bounded rationality in combination with any degree of uncertainty underpins the argument for incomplete contracts—the idea that no contract written can feasibly make provisions for every possible permutation of circumstance, changes in demand, cost, input price, natural disaster, or time. The important implication of incomplete contracts is that a situation will arise that is not provided for in the agreement, and at that time the agreement will need to be renegotiated. Incomplete contracts are a key assumption for the further study of economic organization, but a fairly reasonable one.

A second observation cum assumption about economic agents is that they are opportunistic, and will act in their own best interests for individual gain. This has powerful implications for both contracts and economic organization, contrasted with the implications from bounded rationality, adapted from Williamson (1988):

Williamson (1988) Fundamental Assumption Impacts to Contracts and Organization

	Bounded Rationality	*Opportunism*
Contracts	Contracts necessarily incomplete	Contract as a promise is naive
Economic organization	Exchange facilitated by adaptive decision-making features to cope with incomplete contracts	Trading requires support of safeguards

The final foundational element is the existence of transaction-specific assets, making incomplete contracts and opportunism particularly relevant. A transaction-specific asset is an asset whose value in that transaction exceeds its value in other transactions. Klein, Crawford, and Alchian (1978) called the value difference "quasi-rents," and the problems created by these assets increase as the specificity-induced quasi-rents increase. As transaction-specific investment increases, a bilateral dependency is created: the seller is presented with less and less interesting alternatives to sell his production, and the buyer becomes locked in as purchasing from another (nonspecialized) source presumably becomes cost prohibitive. They characterized vertical integration as a strategy to reduce or eliminate postcontractual opportunistic behavior—that is, the holdup or extortion problem that occurs when the contract needs to be renegotiated and specific assets give buyer and seller unusual market power.

Both transaction cost economics and property rights theory are founded on the principles of these three elements, but with differing predictions and empirical support. An overview of the frameworks follows.

TRANSACTION COST ECONOMICS

The father of transaction cost economics (TCE) is Oliver Williamson. In a series of papers from 1971, 1973, 1979, 1981, and 1988, he outlined and continued to refine the framework, receiving substantial empirical support along the way, testing the predicted outcomes of his ideas. It needs to be stated clearly that the TCE framework is a largely verbal model, versus the structured formal model of property rights theory. As such, the costs discussed in TCE are largely inferred rather than measured, a characteristic that may make it unappealing to some. The empirical support for its predictions is quite robust, however, and along with the compelling nature of the argument overcomes any misgivings this author may have.

Transaction cost economics characterizes transactions on three dimensions: (1) frequency, (2) degree and type of uncertainty, and (3) asset specificity. Transaction frequency is generally described as either occasional or recurring, and for the purposes of economic organization analysis only the recurring activities are of particular interest. Uncertainty comes in many forms, usually including technological, volume, and environmental. Asset specificity ranges from nonspecific to idiosyncratic. Examples of purchases fitting varying frequency and asset specificity follow, adapted from Williamson (1979):

Williamson (1979) Characterizing Transaction Frequency and Asset Specificity

	Asset Specificity		
Frequency	*Nonspecific*	*Mixed*	*Idiosyncratic*
Occasional	Standard equipment	Custom equipment	Build a factory
Recurring	Standard materials	Custom materials	Site-specific transfer of intermediate materials

Williamson (1981) elaborated on the concept of asset specificity, suggesting that it can take one of three forms: (1) site specificity, (2) physical asset specificity, or (3) human capital (skill) specificity. Specificity is the key implied cost driver in TCE, for two reasons: First, in the presence of opportunism and incomplete contracts, the holdup problem and incentives for a trading partner to induce a holdup problem become significantly greater. Vertical integration or long-term flexible contracts are predicted in these cases to protect from opportunism. Second, Williamson (1981) describes a "fundamental transformation" that takes place in the market after a bid has been awarded for transactions with high asset specificity, that other bidders disappear—

again an opportunism problem in which the contract initially is bid in a competitive environment, but when renegotiation comes up, the initial winner has established such a base of specific (and presumably advantaged) assets that others choose not to compete.

The basic prediction of TCE is that recurring transactions, utilizing idiosyncratic or highly specific assets, will tend to be performed within the firm rather than through a market. The key problem for TCE is that it is largely inferential: how does one measure the cost of a (possible) future holdup problem? The costs of uncertainty? Beyond the costs of contracting, negotiation and writing, monitoring, enforcing, and resolution of breaches, very little is explicit in the TCE framework. The empirical literature will deal with this more completely.

PROPERTY RIGHTS THEORY

The property rights theory (PRT) has evolved as a formal model of economic behavior attempting to interconnect ownership rights and incentives. The framework was first laid out by Jensen and Meckling (1976), attempting to understand the conflicts of interest that might exist within the bounds of a firm.

Their first observation is that a firm is made up of agents, each with its own utility-maximizing objective that is not necessarily consistent with the profit-maximizing objective of the firm. That organizations are often legal fictions designed to act as a nexus for contracts between individuals leads to an increased importance of ownership, which can be described as possessing the rights of control of an asset (capital or human) not specifically assigned in a contract. The incentive effects of ownership are basically the profit-maximizing objectives, and an important implication of the PRT framework is that firms, made up of agents, are not actually profit-maximizing entities.

Two observations follow from this framework: first, that alignment of managements' incentives and monitoring of managements' actions are expensive, and will be performed only up to the point where the marginal benefit to ownership equals the marginal cost of additional incentives/monitoring. A second observation is that modern corporations with typically diffuse ownerships have an even greater problem aligning and monitoring managements' actions via boards of directors, thereby exacerbating agency issues and increasing the costs of organization.

Grossman and Hart (1986) tried to address vertical integration within the PRT framework by setting up a robust "black box" model of the utility maximizing behavior of the firms' agents, describing integration as driven by a desire to control residual rights left over from incomplete contracts. They acknowledge that vertical integration is not costless, particularly in the distortions in incentives for both acquiring and acquired firms, where either/both may have been more efficiently aligned with a profit-maximizing objective prior to integration. Fundamentally, they argue, integration doesn't eliminate the costs of contracting, but only shifts the opportunities for holdup problems.

Hart and Moore (1990) looked more carefully at employee (human) assets, the extent to which investment was required in those assets to perform tasks specific to the firm, and the implications for vertical integration. One advantage to owned human assets is that they can be selectively invested in or fired, whereas a contracted capability (firm) can only be fired as a whole. Again, based on the holdup problem of specific assets, vertical integration is predicted to be more prevalent in situations where profitability is particularly sensitive to access to employees or unique assets.

Whinston (2003) reviewed the empirical literature of the previous two decades supporting EO, and although the theories of TCE and PRT are based on the same principles of bounded rationality, opportunism, and specific assets, he found no support for PRT's detailed predictions in the EO literature.

This result was based partly on the lack of sufficient data to test the predictions of PRT, and secondly on some fundamental differences between PRT and TCE. Where TCE focuses on the quasi-rents associated with asset specificity, PRT deals more specifically on the marginal returns to noncontractible assets (residual rights of control especially to individuals, and the returns thereon). A second observation is that although the predicted results are often in the same direction, toward or away from integration, PRT's prediction is dependent on the changes in marginal returns under different ownership structures, whereas TCE focuses more narrowly on the appropriation of quasi-rents from economic activity.

Overall, PRT is an important framework in the analysis of economic organization, and an interesting one to consider. Although PRT is appealing from a technical standpoint, given the formality and rigor applied to the modeling of individual behavior, the detail and sophistication of its predictions and models make it extremely difficult to apply in practice or test empirically. Agency issues will from here be considered under the construct of opportunism, rather than a formal adaptation of property rights theory.

EMPIRICAL SUPPORT

As mentioned earlier, it is particularly difficult to measure costs inferred by TCE factors, and most of the literature focuses on validating the predictions of TCE rather than evaluating the underlying transaction attributes. Three landmark studies are widely credited with validating the TCE framework. These will be discussed in the following paragraphs and then I will touch on a handful of other studies of interest.

Monteverde and Teece (1982) (M&T) were the first to meaningfully tackle the challenge of validating TCE's predictions. Their study of 133 automotive components sourced and manufactured by General Motors (GM) and Ford in 1976 attempted to test the hypothesis that higher quasi-rents would predict greater likelihood of internal production. Importantly, the indicator M&T used to assess the magnitude of quasi-rents was the extent of the engineering effort, arguing that know-how developed during the five-year development process for an automotive platform creates significant supplier switching costs, effectively creating very product- or platform-specific assets and exposing Ford or GM to a possible holdup problem. Two key results from M&T's analysis were (1) support for the hypothesis that a high development effort correlated strongly to a high probability that a product was produced internally, and (2) observing that only components specific to a product or vendor (i.e., noncatalog or nongeneric) were candidates for insourcing at the observed firms.

Masten (1984) studied the organization of production within the aerospace industry, examining make vs. buy decisions for 1,887 components in a major platform. He chose two measures of component specificity: design specificity, the degree to which a component was unique to the product (from unique to adaptable to generic), and site specificity, reflecting grouping of production facilities, another specificity dimension identified by Williamson. Masten also included complexity as an explanatory variable, as a proxy for technological or technical uncertainty—the more complex a component, the more that might go wrong in execution. His results found design specificity and complexity to be significant variables, as well as affirming M&T's finding that alternative uses for a component (nonspecificity) was decisive in making items a "buy."

Joskow (1985) embarked on an analysis to characterize the relationship between coal mines and "mine mouth" (coal-burning) electricity plants. He identifies here a fairly unique situation where the two parties are forced by regulation to remain separate entities, yet they are highly mutually dependent; the coal plant is optimized to burn the specific type of coal expected to come from the seam in the mine to the exclusion of other types, and the mine itself has few (if any) alternative customers for its coal, particularly given the high transportation costs associated with moving coal. Joskow identifies two types of uncertainty that unquestionably make complete contracts impossible: (1) the utility's projected demand for coal over the 35-year useful life of the plant, and (2) the coal plant's projected mining costs and coal quality over the 35 years. The important result of this study is consistency with the predictions of TCE—that these relationships are characterized by extensive, long-term (all over 20 years), mutually beneficial, and flexible contracts designed to guarantee protection for both sides, align incentives, minimize price haggling, and avoid costly litigation.

Other empirical contributions of note include Walker and Weber (1984). In an analysis of 60 make vs. buy decisions at an automotive components division, they introduced a measure of supplier competition to their model, which had significant impact along with volume uncertainty. Their treatment of the supplier competition result was fairly cursory, but it could be taken as evidence of a (lack of) Williamson's "fundamental transformation" whereby a supplier market is wiped out by the first mover's specific assets advantage, and thus an indication of the low level of specific assets required to compete in this market-place. They further refined their findings in a 1987 paper examining another 60 make vs. buy decisions, more specifically finding that in the presence of high volume uncertainty, there is a tendency to buy in high-competition input markets and to make where there is only limited competition. In both studies, cost considerations were overwhelmingly dominant in the make vs. buy decisions.

In a study of multinational corporations (MNCs), Gatignon and Anderson (1988) contributed an analysis of different types of uncertainty to the ownership (and inferred control) structure of foreign subsidiaries. Country risk was found to be significant, convincing MNCs to take low ownership stakes. Notably, experience managing in foreign countries increased the level of control—some degree of management uncertainty apparently was avoided. Proprietary knowledge was also found to be a keystone in the control equation, as they found it extremely difficult to transfer without direct control.

Finally, John and Weitz (1988) examined behaviors of forward integration into distribution, and came up with results entirely consistent with TCE. First, as human assets in the sales channel required more training (becoming more specific), firms moved to in-house or direct sales. Second, as downstream uncertainty increased, leading to a greater likelihood of renegotiation, firms moved to eliminate the third party (distribution) and deal directly with customers. John and Weitz also found evidence that increased monitoring costs (performance becoming harder to measure) drove firms to internalize.

TCE-driven relationships are not a simple question of make vs. buy, or total vertical integration vs. disintegration. Situations will arise where we may observe ownership, but more frequently real-world problems involve degrees of control over operations and assets. These can range from complete ownership to none at all. In some instances, extremely complex and long-term contracts (even with no ownership interest) are sufficient indicators and appropriate responses to high transaction costs.

More generally, there are some more readily observable attributes to which we can attribute high-TCE characteristics.

Uncertainty associated with volume, technology, management, execution, or environmental factors, which would make contract renegotiation more likely, is a broad-stroke high-TCE indicator.

Specificity indicators all increase the quasi-rents by either increasing economic usefulness in the existing role (investment) or reducing the effective value in alternative applications (precluding other uses).

- *Complexity.* High levels of development effort may result in some indirect investment in the human resources of a firm, in building the architecture knowledge through the development process.

- *Training.* High levels of training in an organization are a direct investment in the HR of a firm's economic activity, whether inside or outside. Processes requiring high skill specialization or knowledge acquisition raise the value of these resources.

- *Uniqueness.* A product or skill set with only one use or extremely limited uses imply a degree of mutual dependency.

- *Switching costs.* Vestige of past investment indicates that the process requires nongeneric capabilities to be performed economically.

- *Supplier competition.* Williamson's "fundamental transformation" suggests that first-move advantages can wipe out specialized marketplaces. Limited or no competition in input markets indicates potentially high switching costs.

- *Site.* An obvious indicator of specificity, site location may preclude transactions with other parties or may allow transactions with many parties.

- *Mutual dependence.* Situations where both partners' livelihood depends on the continued operation of the other brings elements of uncertainty together with specificity, implying very high transaction costs.

Management Literature

Management literature runs the gamut from leadership stories in fish markets to autobiographies of egomaniacal icons. There is an arbitrary separation here between the management and strategy literatures; discussions related to particular decisions have been classified as "management" whereas prescriptions for firm positioning, allocation of resources, and capabilities are considered under "strategy." The management literature that is of particular interest to the study of outsourcing deals particularly with the make vs. buy decision faced by firms over time and tries to be more prescriptive in developing management insight. This body of work borrows heavily from the automotive sector, both because of that sector's wide-ranging, multitiered effects and because it is a fairly captive, observable group of firms to study. Two major themes emerged that are important to the study of make vs. buy decisions: (1) a specific skills-based analysis of appropriateness of outsourcing, and (2) an observation and framework about how and why the optimal vertical integration strategy changes over time.

Fine and Whitney (F&W) (1996) looked at the process of delivering products and services as essentially a systems engineering problem. In their view, the skills central to a firm's success are not necessarily those directly involved in the product or process, but rather complete systems understanding—allowing effective decomposition of product elements and not creating a dependency trap for knowledge. The characteristics they identified to help evaluate a firm's systems engineering capability are identified in Figure 7.1.

F&W's worst-case scenario for outsourcing is where a firm is dependent for knowledge on an element that is integral to the functioning of its product. In their systems engineering lan-

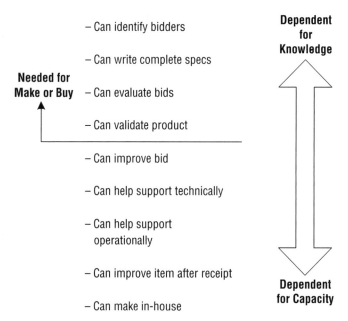

Figure 7.1   Fine & Whitney (1996) Systems Engineering Capability

guage *integral* means an element is not easily bounded, nor its interconnects easily mapped and specified. They characterize the opportunity for outsourcing by an item's decomposability versus the firm's particular dependency in a useful matrix, adapted in Figure 7.2.

This specific skills– and specific knowledge–based framework is analogous to asset specificity in the TCE framework, where the problems envisioned by F&W are very much more detailed holdup problems described by Williamson. Their

Matrix of Dependency and Outsourcing

	Dependent for Knowledge	Dependent for Capacity
Outsourced Item Is Decomposible	Potential Outsourcing Trap Your partners could supplant you.They have as much or more knowledge and can obtain the same elements you can.	Best Outsourcing Opportunity You understand it, you can plug it into your process or product, and it probably can be obtained from several sources. It probably does not represent competitive advantage in and of itself, buying it means you save attention to put into areas where you have competitive advantage, such as integrating other things
Outsourced Item Is Integral	Worst Outsourcing Situation You don't understand what you are buying or how to integrate it. The result could be failure because you will spend so much time on rework or rethinking.	Can Live with Outsourcing You know how to integrate the item so you may retain competitive advantage even if others have access to the same item.

Figure 7.2   Fine and Whitney (1996) Dependency and Outsourcing

work provides substantially more detailed and less generic language with which to consider the insourcing or outsourcing of an element.

The second important construct from the management literature recognizes that optimal economic organization changes and evolves over time. Harrigan (1986) evaluated 192 firms' behavior from 1960 to 1981, examining the tendencies of both successful and unsuccessful firms in changing competitive environments. She observed strong consistency across industries in the nature of vertical integration observed in successful firms at different times in their industries' life cycle. Her observations are largely consistent with TCE, such as successful firms integrating upstream when uncertainty over quality or product complexity cannot be tolerated. An interesting dimension that Harrigan observes, which TCE does not spell out explicitly, is the behavior of successful firms in young industries in the face of high levels of technological uncertainty; here she notes that these (successful) firms developed strong sales/distribution infrastructure in the market's infancy, developing strong ties and relationships with customers as the market evolved.

Charles Fine (1997) added a more complete framework or story about why industries cycle between vertically integrated and modular architectures. From a systems engineering perspective, supporting a vertically integrated integral product architecture requires substantial in-house knowledge, often built around a notion of core competencies. When a market changes quickly, these competencies become rigidities, which pressures a firm to look outside for new ideas. Difficulties managing the development process and staying in the lead in an increasingly complex and new product environment also put pressure on the firm to look outside for "best in world" technologies and systems. Firms with a very strong grasp of the product realization process feel the pressure somewhat less. In a modular architecture, such as today's personal computer (PC) industry, the product is highly separable and easily outsourced. Personal computer makers today find their suppliers' skills for operating systems or graphic subsystems markedly superior to their own, depending on these suppliers completely and enabling competitors to easily replicate their product offerings. Similarly, commoditized component modules make imitation relatively easy, and this ease of access puts significant pressure on profits—all of which add up to a firm feeling pressure to find some way to develop a proprietary and integrated product solution that cannot be easily imitated by competitors. The author's rendition of Fine's flow diagram is shown in Figure 7.3.

Fine's dynamic instability can also be thought of as both sides of a TCE problem—from the marginal architecture side, firms are subject to all manners of holdup problems attributable to their dependence on those suppliers and the market power the firms have ceded. On the integral architecture side, the construct provides us the framework to consider the downside to vertical integration in TCE including: (1) cutoff from the outside

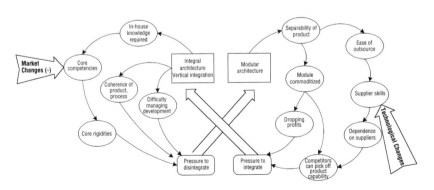

Figure 7.3 Fine (1997) Dynamic Instability

world and possibly latest technology/market advances, (2) diseconomies of scope, problems associated with managing a
wide-ranging base of product- and process-engineering capabilities, and (3) exacerbating possible problems associated with ex-
cess capacity and plant size imbalances.

Strategy Literature

Three meaningful and substantial topics in strategy have
evolved over the past 25 years suited to analysis of outsourcing: (1) Porter's (1980) industry analysis frameworks, helping
to map the competitive landscape, (2) core competencies, first
developed by Prahalad and Hamel (P&H) (1990), and (3) ex-
tension into strategic assets, fostered by Amit and Schoemaker (1993).

Porter's Five Forces framework has become required reading
for most MBA strategy courses, Wharton Executive MBA
(WEMBA) included. The framework helps particularly in identifying market failures and places where industries depart from
traditionally competitive markets. This literature of industry
analysis sparked a craze for firms to identify and utilize competitive advantage, firm-specific, difficult-to-imitate capabilities
that could differentiate their product offerings from others in
the marketplace.

Prahalad and Hamel coalesced a decade's worth of thought
around industry analysis and sustainable competitive advantage, and in so doing coined what would become the favorite
buzzwords of consultants the world over: core competencies.
They moved beyond generic competitive strategies to exploit
market imperfections to try to articulate the fingerprint of a corporation that would make it successful. This fingerprint would

be made up of the collective learning and experience of the organization, its ability and methods of organizing work and delivering value, and the manner in which it communicated across organizational boundaries. P&H implored managers to carefully inventory the skills and capabilities of their organizations to identify core competencies, which could be recognizable by elements that provided potential access to a wide variety of markets, made a significant contribution to customer value, and were hard for competitors to imitate. Although this seems remarkably similar to our (current) common thoughts about competitive advantage, P&H offered the first set of characteristics that could help firms (and consultants) to identify their core competencies.

Where P&H stepped away from the industry analysis framework almost entirely, Amit and Schoemaker tried to tie together industry factors with the resources and capabilities of the firm to help managers identify strategic assets that they believed provided the basis for competitive advantage. In their view, the fundamental management challenge is to identify, develop, protect, and deploy the resources and capabilities of the firm for competitive advantage. Figure 7.4 is adapted from their 1993 article.

Cappelli and Crocker-Hefter (C&C-H) (1996) round out the strategy literature considered here. Their article expands on core competencies and strategic assets, focusing on the distinctive HR capabilities of the firm. The HR-centric world view holds people management as a driver to create and manage core competencies that ultimately differentiate products and drive competitiveness. Not all that dissimilar from the basic notion of core competencies put forward by P&H, the tie to the TCE framework here is that people are, to a large degree, the specific assets of the firm. C&C-H ask managers to consider

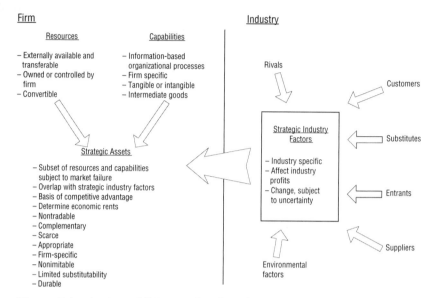

Figure 7.4   Amit and Schoemaker (1993) Genesis of Strategic Assets

the management of those assets as carefully as they watch other activities.

Business Cases

Common threads run throughout the frameworks already described. For the purposes of the business case analyses, I use TCE as the basic platform for characterizing the transactions and setting the backdrop for both outsourcing and insourcing decisions, examining uncertainty factors and specificity. Evidence of opportunism or agency issues will be taken as holdup problems in action.

"Things change" is certainly a generic statement, capturing all manner of temporal issues. As best as possible, I will try to identify changes in the TCE elements (or the emphasis thereon) that led to a change in business direction. The cases that follow do not reflect a lot of evidence of dynamic instability related to competitive markets or evolving architectures.

Core capabilities or a notion of differentiating elements about which no uncertainty can be tolerated will be examined as well. It is difficult to narrowly identify a single element as being at the core of large and diverse organizations; I will try to avoid doing so. However, exposure to potentially business-crippling uncertainty (core functions without substitute and without which the business cannot function) can be identified and the reduced tolerance for uncertainty inferred.

KNOWLES ELECTRONICS— CIRTEK SEMICONDUCTOR

In 1999, Knowles Electronics outsourced a highly proprietary subassembly process to Cirtek Semiconductor, a chip packaging contractor based in Manila, Philippines. After three years of production, Knowles insourced this work to its factory in Penang, Malaysia, in 2003.

The process produces miniature diaphragms for its hearing-aid microphones, well over 12 million per year. The diaphragms are formed by precisely tensioning gold-plated Mylar film and literally gluing the tensioned film onto precision brass rings less than 0.007 of an inch thick with a combination of heat and a proprietary blend of specialty adhesives. Knowles is the larger of only two companies in the world to use diaphragms of this quality level, producing over 85 percent of hearing-aid microphones globally. Knowles developed all the equipment and process technology itself, from the process to gold-plate the Mylar film to the tensioning and gluing (forming) stations to the adhesive mixture and the test equipment at the end of the line. With the embedded experience of developing, building, and maintaining the process, Knowles' equipment and process engineers developed extensive expertise and understanding of the idiosyncrasies in the process. In 1999, Knowles' engineering team averaged over 15 years of service with the company.

From a TCE perspective, this is clearly a recurring transaction. Uncertainty takes several forms: (1) volume uncertainty, (2) management uncertainty at Knowles' own sites, (3) technological uncertainty and (4) environmental uncertainty. The means for production are about as specific as can be—quasirents associated with the production assets comprise virtually the full value of the product with no productive alternative use for the equipment. The diaphragm-forming process hits virtually all the indicators for specificity identified earlier—highly complex, requiring high levels of training, unique to Knowles, high switching costs should a change be desired, no supplier competition, and some mutual dependence. The product size alleviates most site specificity concerns, because transportation time and cost (via airfreight) are relatively small.

With all the TCE factors lined up as highly idiosyncratic and screaming for vertical integration, why would Knowles even consider outsourcing this process to a third party, as it ultimately did? The TCE assessment may be a little harsh, where the Fine-Whitney matrix of dependency might categorize this as a livable outsourcing relationship, dependent for capacity on an integral component—especially given that Knowles retained virtually all the engineering resources that built both the equipment and the process.

Three considerations carried the decision to move production outside. First, cost savings was a very real pressure to Knowles, and Illinois versus Manila offered nearly $1 million annual savings. Second, management uncertainty/instability at Knowles' facility in Malaysia became an issue. Two iterations of turnover in the most senior position in Knowles' Penang facility created misgivings within management about whether introducing this highly complex, sensitive process to a factory struggling to get on track made sense. Finally, control arrangements, including continuous U.S. engineering support and presence in Manila for the first year as well as the addition of permanent-resident quality engineering support at Cirtek's facility, convinced Knowles that it would retain sufficient control of the process that delivery uncertainty could be avoided.

After three years of relatively successful production, Knowles faced unraveling this relationship. Several features had changed substantially, but cost savings was again the overriding impetus for insourcing the activity. Knowles estimated up to $500,000 in savings annually from moving the process into its facility in Malaysia on an incremental basis. All four uncertainty variables identified earlier changed significantly: Knowles experienced a substantial upswing in its business, straining all of its production facilities and in particular diaphragm production—Cirtek's inability to commit to ramping up quickly cost Knowles in missed deliveries. Knowles management situation in Malaysia stabilized after three failed general managers; the current leader of the organization provided calm and professionalism to the entire team giving corporate management increased confidence that they could handle the added work. Technological uncertainty became an issue, whereas previously the process was believed stable. Knowles found itself nearing breakthroughs in dramatically improving the process with new epoxies and forming processes, and these changes would be substantially easier to implement with internal organization. Finally, the environmental uncertainty became worrisome, with Filipino politics becoming increasingly unstable and demonstrations and riots taking place frequently in downtown Manila. Cirtek also began showing signs of opportunism; the rest of their business had deteriorated between 2000 and 2002, and Knowles' business became very nearly the sole source of revenue. Though Knowles approached Cirtek on multiple occasions to discuss process-improvement opportunities and cost-down initiatives, it was rebuffed each time; Cirtek was unwilling or unable to implement or share any cost improvements with Knowles.

Ultimately, the changes in uncertainty drove Knowles to shift its strategy from outsource to internal organization, though in both decisions cost played a major role. This is consistent with Walker-Weber's findings that cost tends to dominate other variables in firms' decision-making processes. Reluctance to further invest in an overseas facility pending further experience with its management is similar to Gatignon-Anderson's findings on the behavior of MNCs. The importance of uncertainty is also consistent with the strategic assets construct: diaphragm production is a core product element, integral to the performance of its microphones, that it cannot live without. Industry structure also played a key role in the sensitivity to uncertainty; Knowles is made more sensitive to delivery and schedule considerations as it defends a dominant market-share position in a niche industry. Where Knowles was able (rightly or wrongly) to convince itself that it had mitigated uncertainty considerations in making the decision to outsource, the tides clearly shifted against the move, leading to the decision to insource.

JPMC—IBM

In December 2002, JP Morgan Chase (JMPC) and IBM signed a record seven-year IT outsourcing pact for large elements of its data processing infrastructure, worth over $5 billion in revenues to IBM. In September 2004, JPMC and IBM announced the termination of this pact and the transfer back of over 4,000 employees to JMPC from IBM.

The outsourcing pact was not a complete transfer of JPMC IT capabilities outside, but limited to management of its data centers, help desks, distributed computing, data networks, and voice networks. JPMC elected to retain application development and delivery, as well as desktop support in-house. The most widely cited reasons for the outsourcing initiative were: absolute cost savings, cost variability (convert fixed costs into somewhat variable expenses), access to IBM's research and innovation, improved service levels, higher capacity, and opportunities for employees.

The limitation of the scope of work transferred outside is important, both because it defines the transactions as continuous (extremely frequent) and because it provides some insight into management's thinking during the outsourcing decision by making these elements discrete—from a systems engineering perspective, decomposable. This also apparently limited the specific nature of the assets involved, because employees were transferred wholesale, all of the embedded knowledge was retained, and the functions themselves were fairly generic and nonspecific to JPMC. The Fine-Whitney matrix would classify this as a potential trap, with the potential for JPMC to lose touch (from an already weak position) with the underlying technology involved in its data processing centers. Transferring applications development and deployment would have been highly specific, given its idiosyncratic nature. The work transferred appeared relatively low specificity against the indicators: complexity and site specificity would seem to be the only high-TCE attributes. The basic technologies and processes were not unique to JPMC; there were presumably several large-scale partners JPMC could have chosen for the contract. All 4,000 employees remained on-site, mitigating any site-specificity effects.

The uncertainty that management appeared to emphasize in making the outsourcing decision was related to technology, management, and volume. The technology spin here is that JPMC does not appear to believe itself "best in world" at data center management or technology, whereas IBM makes this a core focus of its R&D and is better able to keep up and lead as innovation progresses. Management uncertainty is twofold: first, the service level problems that led JPMC to believe that a service level agreement with an outside party would be more effective at guaranteeing performance, and second, an admission that IBM brings best in world management processes (Universal Management Infrastructure), which JPMC implicitly did not believe it could develop or implement on its own. JPMC also seemed to value turning these IT management expenses from a fixed cost into a semivariable cost, though, I believe, the higher capacity and flexible capability arguments are more related to IBM's marketing of on-demand services than specific valuable gains for JPMC.

Pundits attribute JPMC's decision to unwind this agreement largely to the new chief operating officer Jamie Dimon, arriving as a result of a megamerger with Bank One. There may be some basis for this opinion, as Dimon has been widely quoted as saying, "I don't believe in outsourcing." He is also responsible for canceling a similar outsourcing pact between Bank One and IBM/AT&T in 2002. Williamson (1973) even allows for individual preferences, atmosphere, and a role in make vs. buy decisions (though he does not mention it again). Although it is likely that Dimon's predilection for insourcing was a major driver of the decision, several other important attributes and organizational emphases changed as well.

The merger of JPMC and Bank One changed JPMC substantially, and particularly in the area of IT. Where JPMC struggled to synchronize its technology base and keep current with the best systems, Bank One had recently spent $500 million to standardize and centralize its IT systems, and another $150 million on a state-of-the-art data center. Almost overnight JPMC moved from struggling to keep up to best in world data center capabilities. Other factors remained largely the same, though evidence of opportunism began to surface. Melissa Davis, WEMBA 29 and former vice president in IT at JPMC, had this to say:

> The service level of the technologists went from horrible in JPMC to horrible when they were part of IBM. I don't have much hope that they'll be any better when they come back to JPMC. . . . Although there were concerns with the move, one comment I heard was that [transferred employees] weren't expected to work as hard at IBM—if it wasn't in the JPMC/IBM contract, they wouldn't do the work and their managers at IBM supported that.

Uncertainty factors were clearly diminished, between JPMC's newfound tech leadership position and validation that IBM was no better at providing service functions, JPMC apparently had little to gain from continuing the relationship. There is an important element of the JPMC rationale that underpins Dimon's strong belief in internal organization, the ability to control his own destiny for a capability he viewed as "core, like your spine," a feeling exacerbated by the highly competitive, scale-sensitive, and recently merger-crazy banking industry. This is most likely the impetus behind the decision, ultimately, that the internal organization offers more control and correspondingly less uncertainty in many ways than contracting for services.

KNOWLES ELECTRONICS—
STAMPED METAL PARTS

From 2001 to 2003, Knowles Electronics worked with two stamping companies in Taiwan and China to develop their capability to produce ultraprecision components for its hearing-aid microphones and speakers. In 2004, Knowles elected to terminate this initiative in favor of setting up its own facility in Penang, Malaysia.

Knowles uses well over 100 million stamped metal parts per year. These parts are generally made of extremely high grades of stainless steel and specialty nickel-iron alloys, and most have features that are controlled to ±0.001 of an inch tolerances, many as narrowly as ±0.0001 of an inch. In addition to being quite small and precise, Knowles combines "deep draw" techniques to form cups and tubes with a proprietary shearing process that makes a perfectly square edge that is suited to welding. No other high-volume, deep-draw stamping components require such a precise, square edge. Stamping dies to make these components are run and maintained in house. Most were designed and assembled internally as well, with die-element manufacturing done both internally and externally. Generally, each stamped part is made on a single die that may make other parts as well, but redundancy is very limited.

Many of the business considerations around this outsourcing decision are similar to the earlier Cirtek diaphragm-forming decision, specifically Knowles' market position and sensitivity to interruptions in supply. From a technological base, it was Knowles' intention to eliminate its internal capability for tool and die design and maintenance support. This shifts its dependency dangerously close to knowledge for an integral component—the worst possible outsourcing situation according to

Fine and Whitney. Confounding this categorization, however, was Knowles' extensive experience with tool and die maintenance and construction and in-house capability, leading it to believe that it could provide start-up and troubleshooting expertise to the selected partners.

The dependency element also hinges on the perspective of Knowles' management. There was widespread feeling at program inception that, at the end of the day, the stamping process was a fairly generic one, controllable through well-understood statistical processes, and low-risk in execution. Extensive supplier competition heightened this feeling, as a broad stamped parts supply base bid aggressively for the work. Metal stamping technology has not had a major innovation in the past several decades, and overall precision carbide die maintenance is fairly well understood. The essential argument here is around both the parts and the technology: Are the parts modular components or integral to the functioning of the device? Are there enough specific-to-Knowles attributes that this is a unique technology, or is this a commoditized offering? Management here chose to be convinced that metal parts were a modular component produced using a common manufacturing process.

Specific assets gave Knowles some pause, as each die was unique and parts ran exclusively in one die; catastrophic failure in a die could be crippling. Mitigating this risk was to have the two partner firms each build duplicate dies of their own as they became qualified and competent at each part, effectively doubling the number of dies available and allowing Knowles to warehouse its existing dies at local stamping shops. Other specificity indicators were fairly neutral; partners were expected to have already invested in their own skills and only have to learn the intricacies of Knowles' own parts. Site specificity is also not an issue in transporting these small parts.

OUTSOURCING

All told, the outsourcing program was a miserable failure. Two years of effort in an almost but not quite getting there campaign, and Knowles was ready for an internal transfer. Cost considerations dictated that its production facility in Illinois be closed, and internal transfer now seemed the best route for several reasons. First, there was far more embedded knowledge than was anticipated. During the course of the outsourcing effort it was discovered that not a single die had a complete set of accurate documentation, effectively grinding any die duplication to a halt. This is precisely the nonpatentable, firm-specific knowledge Monteverde and Teece believed drove high switching costs; rebuilding that knowledge, once gained, is exceptionally difficult—more so in a potential holdup situation. This knowledge was a key factor in pushing Knowles to set up its own capability in Malaysia.

Internal organization was chosen for several other reasons as well. Alchian-Demsetz's information and monitoring costs, understanding the health of the operation and the quality processes, are substantially lower internally. This is an explicit transactions cost which is greatly reduced with an internal operation. Volume uncertainty became an issue, driven by the same business upswing that put pressure on Cirtek's ability to deliver. Knowles made a commitment to buy additional presses as part of the transfer initiative, increasing total press capacity by nearly 50 percent. The final element that drove Knowles to set up its own capability came when two employees volunteered for multiyear expatriate assignments, and two others agreed to live in Malaysia until the end of 2004. The expats along with other benefits associated with internal organization gave Knowles a strong sense of control over a critical and strategic means of production.

Conclusion

Based on these three vignettes, uncertainty appears to play a much larger role in real-world decision making than the frameworks presented earlier. Individual assessments of core and business-critical elements appear to make firms that much more careful in managing the assets of their businesses. At some level, the importance of uncertainty is reasonable given that asset specificity considerations are unchanged; uncertainty becomes the de facto swing variable. Setting the predictions of property rights theory aside, managers will ultimately do what they feel is best for their firm, and it is not at all inconsistent with the academic and business literature to say that this is a highly subjective practice determined not by formulaic rules or inferred costs, but by perspectives and emphasis. Harrigan described the genesis of vertical integration strategies not as a single make-buy decision but rather as a combination of decisions, ultimately made up of the views of the firms' management of the industry trends, the resources and capabilities of the firm, and the many factors of uncertainty that can affect firm performance. In the examples described, management's beliefs about the appropriate responses to uncertainty became driving forces in both the outsourcing and insourcing decisions.

In the end, the task of managers is to make decisions based on their uncertain vision of the future. Those who are most right and make the best positioning decisions will tend to be the most successful. The stories presented here have attempted to provide some insight into the perspectives and rationales applied to both the decision to outsource as well as reversal of that decision, with a backdrop of meaningful economic, management, and strategic frameworks.

References

Accelerator Group. 2004. Impact of offshore outsourcing on the manufacturing sector in Michigan and the United States. June.

Alchian, A., and H. Demsetz. 1972. Production, information costs, and economic organization. *American Economic Review* 62(5): 777–795.

Amit, R., and P. Schoemaker. 1993. Strategic assets and organizational rent. *Strategic Management Journal* 14(1):33–46.

Cappelli, P., and A. Crocker-Hefter. 1996. Distinctive human resources are firms' core competencies. *Organizational Dynamics* 24(3):6–23.

Casale, F. 2000. Our vendors, ourselves. *CIO* 1(November 1).

Clark, D. 2004. Another lure of outsourcing: Job expertise. *Wall Street Journal* (April 12):B1.

Coase, R. 1937. The nature of the firm. *Economica New Series* 4(16):386–405.

Dyer, J. 1996. Specialized supplier networks as a source of competitive advantage: Evidence from the auto industry. *Strategic Management Journal* 17:271–291.

Dyer, J., and W. Chu. 1997. The economic value of trust in supplier-buyer relations. Working Paper W-0145a (November).

Dyer, J., P. Kale, and H. Singh. 2004. When to ally and when to acquire. *Harvard Business Review* (July–August):108–115.

Economist. 2004. Survey of outsourcing (November 11).

Fine, C. n.d. Power diffusion in automotive supply chains. FY '97 International Motor Vehicle Program Working Paper.

Fine, C., G. Gilboy, and G. Parker. 1995. Technology supply chains: An introductory essay. MIT Working Draft (May).

Fine, C., and D. Whitney. 1996. Is the make-buy decision a core competence? Sloan Working Paper 3875 WP 140–96 (January).

Furubotn, E., and S. Pejovich. 1972. Property rights and economic theory: A survey of recent literature. *Journal of Economic Literature* 10(4):1137–1162.

Gatignon, H., and E. Anderson. 1988. The multinational corporation's degree of control over foreign subsidiaries: An empirical test of a transaction cost explanation. *Journal of Law, Economics, and Organization* 4(2):305–333.

Grossman, S., and O. Hart. 1986. The costs and benefits of ownership: A theory of vertical and lateral integration. *Journal of Political Economy* 94(4):691–719.

Hancox, M., and R. Hackney. 2000. IT outsourcing: Frameworks for conceptualizing practice and perception. *Information Systems Journal* 10:217–237.

Harrigan, K. 1986. Matching vertical integration strategies to competitive conditions. *Strategic Management Journal* 7 (November–December):535–555.

Hart, O., and J. Moore. 1990. Property rights and the nature of the firm. *Journal of Political Economy* 98(6):1119–1158.

Helfat, C., and D. Teece. 1987. Vertical integration and risk reduction. *Journal of Law, Economics, and Organization* 3(1):47–67.

Hilsenrath, J. 2004. Data gap. *Wall Street Journal* (April 12):A1.

Jensen, M., and W. Meckling. 1976. Theory of the firm: Managerial behavior, agency costs and ownership structure. *Journal of Financial Economics* 3:305–360.

John, G., and B. Weitz. 1988. Forward integration into distribution: An empirical test of transaction cost analysis. *Journal of Law, Economics, and Organization* 4(2):337–355.

Joskow, P. 1985. Vertical integration and long-term contracts: The case of coal-burning electric generating plants. *Journal of Law, Economics, and Organization* 1(1):33–80.

Joskow, P. 1988. Asset specificity and the structure of vertical relationships: Empirical evidence. *Journal of Law, Economics, and Organization* 4(1):95–117.

Klein, B., R. Crawford, and A. Alchian. 1978. Vertical integration, appropriable rents, and the competitive contracting process. *Journal of Law and Economics* 21(2):297–326.

Masten, S. 1984. The organization of production: Evidence from the aerospace industry. *Journal of Law and Economics* 27(2):403–417.

Monteverde, K., and D. Teece. 1982. Supplier switching costs and vertical integration in the automobile industry. *Bell Journal of Economics* 13(1):206–213.

Novak, S., and S. Eppinger. 2001. Sourcing by design: Product complexity and the supply chain. *Management Science* 47(1): 189–204.

Porter, M. E. 1980. *Competitive strategy: Techniques for analyzing industries and competitors.* New York: Free Press.

Prahalad, C. K., and G. Hamel. 1990. The core competence of the corporation. *Harvard Business Review* (May–June):79–91.

Roodhooft, F., and L. Warlop. 1999. On the role of sunk costs and asset specificity in outsourcing decisions: A research note. *Accounting, Organizations and Society* 24:363–369.

Sako, M., and F. Murray. 1999. Modular strategies in cars and computers. *Financial Times* 12(June).

Spiller, P. 1985. On vertical mergers. *Journal of Law, Economics, and Organization* 1(2):285–312.

Walker, G., and D. Weber. 1987. Supplier competition, uncertainty, and make-or-buy decisions. *Academy of Management Journal* 30(3):589–596.

Walker, G., and D. Weber. 1984. A transaction cost approach to make-or-buy decisions. *Administrative Science Quarterly* 29: 373–391.

Wall Street Journal. 2004. Forrester revises loss estimates to overseas jobs. May 17. A8.

Wall Street Journal. 2004. Offshore face-off. May 10. R6.

Wall Street Journal. 2004. U.S. says 4,633 jobs were lost to "off-shoring" in first quarter. June 10.

Whinston, M. 2003. On the transaction cost determinants of vertical integration. *Journal of Law, Economics & Organization* 19(1):1–24.

Williamson, O. 1967. Hierarchical control and optimum firm size. *Journal of Political Economy* 75(2):123–138.

Williamson, O. 1971. The vertical integration of production: Market failure considerations. *American Economic Review* 61:112–123.

Williamson, O. 1973. Markets and hierarchies: Some elementary considerations. *American Economic Review* 63(2):316–325.

Williamson, O. 1979. Transaction-cost economics: The governance of contractual relations. *Journal of Law and Economics* 22(2):233–261.

Williamson, O. 1981. The modern corporation: Origins, evolution, attributes. *Journal of Economic Literature* 19(December): 1537–1568.

Williamson, O. 1988. The logic of economic organization. *Journal of Law, Economics, and Organization* 4(1):65–93.

Williamson, O. 1996. Economics and organization: A primer. *California Management Review* 38(2):131–146.

JP Morgan Chase Research

Special thanks to Melissa Davis, WEMBA 29 and former VP-IT at JPMC.

ABC News. 2004. JP Morgan Chase plans to rehire 4,000. September 15.

CNN Money. 2004. JP Morgan scraps $5bn deal. September 15.

ComputerWorld. 2004. IT outsourcing could be an issue for bank merger. January 19.

ComputerWorld. 2004. JP Morgan Chase to scale back outsourcing pact. June 14.

Evans, B. 2004. Business technology: Outsourcing on the outs at JP Morgan, Wal-Mart. *InformationWeek.* September 20.

IBM Press Release. 2002. JP Morgan Chase signs record outsourcing agreement with IBM. December 31.

IBM White Paper. 2001. Transformational outsourcing. May.

JPMC Internal PowerPoint deck, 2003 Outsourcing Implementation.

Marshall, J. 1999. JP Morgan's evolutionary leap of faith. *Global Investor* (May):3.

McDougall, P. 2004. Bringing it home. *InformationWeek.* September 20.

McDougall, P. 2004. Chase cancels IBM outsourcing deal, true to its president's form. *InformationWeek.* September 15.

Savage, T. 2001. Terry Savage talks money with Jamie Dimon. *Chicago Sun Times.* July 29.

Streeter, B. 2004. Dimon reflections. *ABA Banking Journal.* March.

Wall Street Journal. 2002. IBM cements deal with Deutsche Bank. December 19. A10.

Conclusion

A
lthough anything but new, outsourcing is a major factor in the changing world of work for both organizations and individuals. It does not turn lead into gold, but it is fundamentally transforming how organizations operate, and, as is the case with Nike, completely transforms the work of the organization.

Although outsourcing has empowered and provided opportunities for many, it has also recklessly devastated the lives of millions.

The pace and extent of outsourcing are only going to increase, so it is particularly important that we address any shortcomings now. Embracing five imperatives will improve not just outsourcing but overall organizational performance:

1. Organization leaders should focus on objectives, not strategy.
2. More and better performance metrics must be developed.
3. Organizations should approach *all* resourcing decisions holistically.
4. Human resources should assume responsibility for all human capital aspects of outsourcing.
5. Resourcing decisions should be based on performance.

These five imperatives will also help to make outsourcing ever more operationally transparent, but what must never become transparent are the workers on whom organizations are built.

Glossary of Outsourcing Terms

application service provider (ASP)   A company that offers individuals or enterprises access over the Internet to applications and related services that would otherwise have to be located in their own personal or enterprise computers.

backsourcing   The expiration or termination of an outsourcing arrangement and the recapture in-house of the outsourced function.

baseline   The starting point for defining your needs. As with any metrics, the art of outsourcing comes from defining the relevant parameters.

benchmarking   A method of comparing contract services to market services or other independent standards.

best of breed   Denotes the service provider that is best in its class of services. In contrast, a service provider might not be best of breed but, by reason of superior integration of interoperating services and infrastructures, might provide more valuable services. In selection of a vendor, therefore, the question of whether a best of breed vendor is better than an integrated vendor depends on the customer's actual needs and history as well as on the degree to which the best of breed vendor partners with others in related or complementary fields.

best practices   Those practices and procedures, followed regularly, that reflect the wisdom and experience at leading-edge companies. The collection, interpretation and assembly, and redefinition and updating of best practices historically have been performed by management consultants working in many industries and analyzing common threads. One commentator in an article in *The Wall Street Journal* on October 20, 1998, argued sardonically that best practices are what consultants see while working at one company, repackage, and sell to other corporate clients, touting them as their own.

business-to-business (B2B)   The exchange of products, services, or information between businesses rather than between businesses and consumers.

business-to-consumer (B2C)   The retailing aspect of e-commerce on the Internet. It is often contrasted to business-to-business (B2B) e-commerce.

business-to-employee (B2E)   Internal communications among employees and among different departments provides valuable savings to employees by cutting the cost of printing policy manuals, production manuals, retirement plans, statements of account, and other internal processes. B2E processes may be customized to the enterprise's unique business environment (such as a combination of compliance manuals in a highly regulated industry). B2E can be very generic, involving normal compliance with the plain-vanilla requirements of pension and profit-sharing plans, 401(k) plans, vacation planning, "hotelling" of office space for transient home-based workers, and other emerging business trends.

business process   A sequence of defined steps necessary to achieve a business objective. Business objectives can include any business operation, including product design, marketing, sales, finance, accounting, manufacturing, logistics, supply chain management, customer relationship management, and other special business relationships.

business process outsourcing (BPO)   The procurement of particular services that involve ongoing outsourcing of specific business processes. In certain industries, design, manufacturing, inspection, and logistics may be outsourced. More recently, BPO has come to include internal, back-office functions such as internal audit, finance, billing, accounting, and other operations support. BPO front-office functions may include customer relationship management, with sales, call centers, and fulfillment services.

business process reengineering   Represents planned changes in the manner of conducting a business function, such as information collection and reporting, manufacturing, finance, compliance, or administration.

change control or change management   The set of structures, procedures, and rules governing the adoption and implementation of changes in the commercial or financial relationship between the customer and the service provider.

Clawback   A provision in a contract that requires a party who has taken a benefit to return the benefit due to subsequent conditions. In essence, the benefit was never earned because, in retrospect, the party who got the benefit did not deliver what it had promised and it would be fair, taking into account all the risks and circumstances of the events after the contract was signed, to require return of the benefits. In equity, when a court orders restitution, it normally does so as part of the general rescission of the agreement due to inequitable circumstances that prevented the parties from obtaining the benefit of their bargain. In contracting, a clawback (particularly in outsourcing) adopts the restitution concept without imposing a rescission of the entire contract.

common objects   Models of representations of data that are exchanged among different software applications. Such data are any categories that are capable of being defined by category and by related metadata. For example, a common object may include a customer name, order number, or product (stock keeping unit, or SKU). Although Microsoft applications use "common object brokering" tools to allow the interchange of such common objects using cut-and-paste tools, the emergence of XML (extensible hypertext markup language) expands the portability of common objects across incompatible software applications. The use of XML-based databases extends the utility of Web-based communication among business partners.

competitive insourcing   A process in which internal employees may engage in bidding to compete with competitive, third-party bidders for a defined scope of work.

computing on tap   See **on-demand computing**.

consequential damages   Those elements of damages arising from a breach of contract that are measured by loss of income or lost business opportunities.

control without ownership   The result from well-planned arrangements in which the customer obtains effective use of the resources of the external services provider (otherwise known as magic).

co-sourcing™   A term used by one external services provider to trademark its brand of outsourcing services. See also **smartsourcing; outsourcing**.

customer relationship management (CRM)   A marketing and fulfillment system that usually includes a call center, databases, software, and marketing strategy. Like Enterprise Resource Planning (ERP), CRM initiatives are complex and involve re-design of internal business processes and retraining. Successful contracting for CRM outsourcing requires attention to business as well as technology and legal issues.

end-to-end process   The completion of a business process from beginning to end, including all intermediate steps of data capture, processing, analysis, generation of outputs, and, in some cases, implementation of tasks specified by the logic (algorithm) that defines the business process.

enforceability   The conditions under which the terms, conditions, and obligations of the parties under an agreement will be adopted and confirmed by a court of competent jurisdiction.

enterprise resource planning (ERP)   Software that integrates the various functions of an enterprise based on sharing of data in a common database that, when processed, generates relevant management information for purchasing departments, manufacturing, sales, delivery, and related internal processes (such as HR and accounting). In principle, ERP software is capable of running the enterprise (and multiple enterprises) as an integrated operation.

exchanges   Exchanges utilize the Internet to allow qualified and registered users to look for buyers or sellers of goods and services. Depending on the approach, buyers or sellers may specify prices or invite bids. Transactions can be initiated and completed, and ongoing purchases may qualify customers for volume discounts or special offers.

extranet   Extends the intranet (see **intranet**) to information users from outside the enterprise. Extranets are used to provide access to information that can be used by suppliers, customers, banks and other financial institutions, and others needing access to an enterprise's data.

facilities management   The solution by which the customer entrusts to an external services provider the responsibility for operations and software applications and for the management of the associated instrumentalities (hardware, software, applications programming personnel, etc.), while retaining the general oversight and supervision of its information technology. In broader terms, facilities management may apply to other fields, such as applications maintenance, updating, or revision.

fraud   An intentional deception, for unjust advantage, that causes loss or inconvenience to the party relying on the false or misleading statement. In contract matters, a fraud is the cause of an error bearing on a material part of the contract.

gain-sharing   A technique for sharing risk and reward on a long-term basis. Euphemistically, gain-sharing is not labeled as risk sharing, so care must be taken to identify what is being shared and why.

grid computing   See **on-demand computing**. The concept of grid comes from the electricity industry. The electrical grid is a network of infrastructure components that generate, transmit, and distribute electricity. By analogy, by flicking a switch, you can have the outsourced business services flow directly and instantly to your office.

homesourcing   The sourcing of services to telecommuters, whether acting as employees (insourcing) or as independent contractors (outsourcing).

indemnification   A method of shifting legal liability from one party to another by contract.

insourcing   The transfer of an outsourced function to an internal department of the customer, to be managed entirely by employees.

intranet   A privately maintained computer network that can be accessed only by authorized persons.

liability   The legal obligation arising out of a failure to honor one's legal liability to another party, such as by contract or in tort.

local area network (LAN)   A group of computers and associated devices that share a common communications line and typically share the resources of a single processor or server within a small geographic area (for example, within an office building). Usually, the server has applications and data storage that are shared in common by multiple computer users.

managed security services (MSS)   Services that provide indepth analysis to find intrusion threats and respond to security breaches. MSS contains elements such as Web-enabled, real-time security information, best-practice policies, in-depth monitoring, safeguard management capabilities, and strong incident response and computer forensic services.

massive outsourcing   Refers to the process in which a majority of the business support processes are outsourced in one transaction or a small number of related transactions. The purpose of massive outsourcing is to drive shareholder value by shifting to others the operational responsibility for critical operations that do not deliver comparative advantage, or in which the company chooses not to invest due to comparatively low returns on investment.

near shore   Offshore outsourcing within a nearby territory, and accessible by short travel or telephone in the same or neighboring time zone.

offsourcing   Offsourcing (a term we invented) refers to the restructuring of a supply chain where one company relies on its supplier for functions that were previously performed in-house. The offsourced functional unit is able to generate greater value as a part of the supplier's business than in the customer's business. What makes offsourcing so powerful is that the supply chain is tightened by the improved functioning of the offsourced employees in the new environment.

on-demand computing   A form of outsourcing agreement, sometimes called utility computing, grid computing, or computing on tap, that is based on variable payments for variable volumes of variable types of services over a long term that includes at least one refresh cycle for some, if not all, of the underlying technology. Targeted toward enterprise customers, the key element is the scalability of the computing resources—licenses, computers, networks, systems, storage, telecommunications, and asset mangement—that the customer may purchase under the program. The customer's commitment is equivalent to a subscription or requirements purchasing contract, but payment alternatives may run the gamut from a customer's purchase, leasing, or payment "by the use." This does not make the service provider a virtual chief technology officer. Generally, the concept is designed to allow the customer to acquire technology in any manner that suits its individual needs.

outsourcing (or sourcing)   The transfer (or delegation) to an external service provider of the operation and day-to-day management of a business process. The customer receives a service that performs a distinct business function that fits into the customer's overall business operations. Sometimes the process is one that historically has been performed by a vertically integrated enterprise, such as data processing. More recently, outsourcing defines the services sector for those services that were not part of the vertically integrated enterprise, such as telecommunications, web site hosting, transportation services, logistics, and professional services of regulated professionals.

quality of service   A concept that is used to differentiate one provider from another. Typically, the outsourcing customer seeks to enhance its own quality of service by obtaining quality of service from its outsourcing suppliers.

renegotiation   The process of evolution of an existing outsourcing agreement. This process is facilitated through effective design and implementation of contract management processes from inception of the outsourcing relationship.

request for information (RFI)   A document that requests prospective service providers to provide general information on capabilities and their overall business.

request for proposal (or RFP)   A document that requests prospective service providers to propose the terms, conditions, and other elements of an agreement to deliver specified services.

scope   Identifies what is available for sourcing from external service providers.

service level agreement (SLA)   Specifications for services to be delivered. SLAs define the type, value, and conditions of the outsourcing services to be provided. SLAs define the overall relationship by establishing parameters for quality of service.

smartsourcing   A euphemism for the basic challenge of outsourcing as a management technique.

stalking horse   A competitor who never had a meaningful opportunity to win a contract. A stalking horse differs from the losing competitor because the customer intended only to use the stalking horse to generate competitive price quotations and to challenge the preferred provider (who ultimately wins the bidding), and is not compensated for this function. Service providers caught in this role will not succeed in business if they continue to be just stalking horses.

statement of work   Document that sets forth the work to be done.

storage area network (SAN)   A high-speed special-purpose network that interconnects different kinds of data storage devices with associated data servers on behalf of a larger network of users. Typically, a storage area network is part of the overall network of computing resources for an enterprise.

subcontractor   A service provider that is responsible directly to the general contractor and may not have privity of contractual relationship with the outsourcing customer.

supply chain management   An integrated process for managing all levels of the flow of information from an enterprise to its suppliers and customers, including its own internal manufacturing resources.

transfer of undertakings (Protection of Employment) (TUPE)   A law implementing legal rights of employees to continue in the same job if the business unit is transferred.

utility computing   See **on-demand computing**. IBM has attempted to dominate this market by naming its market offering The Next Utility. Buying information technology is supposed to be as easy as flipping a switch.

virtual private network   A network established using telephone lines and/or the Internet to transmit digital information between defined receiving and transmitting stations, such as telephones, computers, and data routing equipment.

wide area network (WAN) A geographically dispersed telecommunications network. The term distinguishes a broader telecommunication structure from a local area network (LAN). A wide area network may be privately owned or rented, but the term usually connotes the inclusion of public (shared user) networks.

Outsourcing Companies and Services

A Look at Some of the Services That Companies Are Outsourcing

Advertising, Marketing, and Public Relations Services
Component Manufacturing
Customer Service Solutions
Document Design Services
Employee Benefits and Administration Services
Facility Engineering and Maintenance
Field Test Services
Food and Cafeteria Services
Graphic Design Services
Human Resources Services
Information Technology Services
Internet Services
Legal Services
Mailroom Services
Payroll Processing Services
Product Warehousing, Distribution, and Delivery
Software Development Services
Telemarketing Services
Travel Services

261

A Look at Some Companies That Are Outsourcing

Accenture
Access Electronics
Adobe Systems
AIG
Alamo Rent A Car
Allstate
Amazon.com
American Express
American Greetings
American Household
American Tool
American Uniform Company
AMETEK
Anheuser-Busch
AOL
Applied Materials
AT&T
Bank of America
Bank of New York
Bank One
Bassett Furniture
Bellsouth
Best Buy
Black & Decker
Boeing
Bose Corporation
Brady Corporation
Briggs Industries
Bristol-Myers Squibb

Bumble Bee
Burlington House Home
   Fashions
Cains Pickles
Capital One
Caterpillar
Charles Schwab
CIBER
Cigna
Circuit City
Cisco Systems
Citigroup
Clorox
Coca-Cola
Columbia House
Comcast Holdings
CompuServe
Computer Associates
Conseco
Continental Airlines
Cross Creek Apparel
Dana Corporation
Davis Wire Corp.
Dayton Superior
Delta Airlines
DIRECTV
Dow Chemical
Dun & Bradstreet
DuPont

Earthlink

Eastman Kodak

Edco, Inc.

Editorial America

Eli Lilly

Elmer's Products

E-Loan

Ernst & Young

Evenflo

Expedia

Fair Isaac

Fawn Industries

Federated Department Stores

Fidelity Investments

First American Title Insurance

First Data

Fluidmaster

Ford Motor Company

Franklin Mint

Frito-Lay

Fruit of the Loom

GE Capital

General Electric

General Motors

Gerber

Gillette

Goodrich

Goodyear Tire & Rubber

Google

Guardian Life Insurance

Haggar

Halliburton

Hamilton Beach/Proctor Silex

Helen of Troy

Hershey

Hewlett-Packard

Home Depot

Honeywell

HSN

IBM

Illinois Tool Works

Infogain

Ingersoll-Rand

Intel

International Paper

Intuit

Iris Graphics, Inc.

Jacobs Engineering

Jacuzzi

Jan Sport

Jockey International

John Crane

John Deere

Johnson & Johnson

Johnson Controls

JP Morgan Chase

Justin Brands

Kaiser Permanente

Kellogg

Kellwood

Key Industries

Kimberly-Clark

OUTSOURCING COMPANIES AND SERVICES

Kraft Foods
Kwikset
LaCrosse Footwear
Lake Village Industries
Lands' End
Lear Corporation
Levi Strauss
Lexmark International
Lockheed Martin
Lowe's
Lucent
Mars, Inc.
Marshall Fields
Master Lock
Maytag
Mellon Bank
Merrill Lunch
MetLife
Microsoft
Midwest Electric Products
Moen
Motorola
Nabisco
National Life
NCR Corporation
Netgear
New World Pasta
Nike
Nordstrom
Northwest Airlines
Office Depot
Ohio Art

Oracle
Orbitz
Otis Elevator
Owens Corning
Palm One
PeopleSoft
PepsiCo
Perot Systems
Pfaltzgraff
Pfizer
Pitney Bowes
Polaroid
Power-One
Priceline.com
Procter & Gamble
Prudential Insurance
Quaker Oats
Quark
Qwest Communications
Radio Flyer
RadioShack
Rayovac
Red Kap
Rogers
Rohm & Haas
RR Donnelley & Sons
Rugged Sportswear
Safeway
Sallie Mae
Samsonite
Sara Lee
SoftBrands

Sonoco Products Co.
Sprint
Stanley Furniture
StarKist Seafood
State Farm Insurance
Sweetheart Cup Company
Synygy
Target
TeleTech
Texaco
Texas Instruments
Time Warner
Toys "Я" Us
TRW Automotive
Tupperware
Tyco International
Union Pacific Railroad
Unisys

United Airlines
United Health Group
United Plastics Group
USAA
Verizon
Vertiflex Products
Vital Sourcing
Wachovia Bank
Walgreens
Walls Industries
Washington Mutual
WebEx
WorldCom
Wyeth
Xerox
Yahoo!
York International
Zenith

Index

INDEX

Index

INDEX

Index

INDEX